Letters

to

Thomas Robert Malthus

on

Political Economy

and

Stagnation of Commerce

by

Jean Baptiste Say

Translated

London, 1821

Contents

© 2011 Booklife (Cover and promotional text)
ISBN 978-1-105-04312-3

ADVERTISEMENT

Mr. Malthus, Professor of Political Economy, at the East India Company's College, has raised himself very high in the literary world by his Essay on Population, which has been translated into all the languages of Europe. For these two years past he has informed us, that he is preparing new *Principles of Political Economy, considered with respect to the practical Applications.* This work, which was impatiently expected, appeared in London, a few months since. M. J. B. Say, who has rendered great services to this science in our Country, and whom we can proudly oppose to the most celebrated English names, has not waited for a French Translation of it[1] to combat those opinions which are in opposition to his.

This discussion, between two men who have proved themselves able, and which is at this moment interesting to all the Trading Interest in the world, has appeared to us worthy the attention of the public, not only under existing circumstances, but at all times.

It will further serve to make Mr. Malthus's work known to those who have not read it.

LETTER I.

Sir,

All those who cultivate the new and beautiful science of Political Economy desire to read the work with which you have just enriched that subject. You are not one of those authors who address the public without having something to inform them; and when to the celebrity of the writer is joined the importance of the subject, when the subject is of no less importance to society, than to inform them what are their means of existence and enjoyment, it is to be supposed that the reader's curiosity must be doubly excited.

I shall not undertake, Sir, to join my suffrage to that of the public, by pointing out everything that is ingenious, and at the same time just, in your work; this would be too great a task. Nor shall I undertake to enter into a discussion with you, upon some points to which you seem to me to attach an importance that they scarcely appear to merit. I shall not here tire either the public or you by dull controversies. But, I say it with sorrow, that there are some fundamental principles discoverable in your doctrine, which, were they to be admitted on so powerful an authority as yours, might cause to retrograde a science, the progress of which you are so good as to assist by your extensive knowledge and talent.

And, in the first place, what fixes my attention, because all the interest of the moment is attached to it, is, from whence comes that general overstock of all the markets of the universe, to which goods are incessantly carried which sell at a loss? -- Whence comes it that in the interior of each state, with a want of action in unison with all the developments of industry, whence comes, I say, that universal difficulty that is experienced in obtaining lucrative employ? And when the cause of this chronic malady is discovered, what are the means of cure? These are questions upon which the happiness and tranquility of nations depend. Wherefore I cannot think a discussion tending to elucidate them will be unworthy your attention, and that of an enlightened public.

All those who, since Adam Smith, have turned their attention to Political Economy, agree that in reality we do not buy articles of consumption with money, the circulating medium with which we pay for them. We must in the first instance have bought this money itself by the sale of our produce.

To a proprietor of a mine, the silver money is a produce with which he buys what he has occasion for. To all those through whose hands this silver afterwards passes, it is only the price of the produce which they themselves have raised by means of their property in land, their capitals, or their industry. In selling them they in the first place exchange them for money, and afterwards they exchange the money for articles of consumption. It is therefore really and absolutely with their produce that they make their purchases: therefore it is impossible for them to purchase any articles whatever, to a greater amount than those they have produced, either by themselves or through the means of their capital or their land.

From these premises I have drawn a conclusion which appears to me evident, but the consequences of which appear to have alarmed you. I had said -- As no one can purchase the produce of another except with his own produce, as the amount for which we can buy is equal to that which we can produce, the more we can produce the more we can purchase. From whence proceeds this other conclusion, which you refuse to admit -- That if certain commodities do not sell, it is because others are not produced, and that it is the raising produce alone which opens a market for the sale of produce.

I know that this proposition has a paradoxical complexion, which creates a prejudice against it. I know that one has much greater reason to expect to be supported by vulgar prejudices, when one asserts that the cause of too much produce is because all the world is employed in raising it.- That instead of continually producing, one ought to multiply barren consumptions, and expend the old capital instead of accumulating new. This doctrine has, indeed, probability on its side; it can be supported by arguments, facts may be interpreted in its favor. But, Sir, when Copernicus and Galileo taught, for the first time, that the sun, although we see it rise every morning in the east, magnificently pass over our heads at noon, and precipitate itself towards the west in the evening, still does not move from its place, they had also universal prejudice against them, the opinions of the Ancients, and the evidence of the senses. Ought they on that account to relinquish those demonstrations which were produced by a sound judgment? I should do you an injustice to doubt your answer.

Besides, when I assert that produce opens a vent for produce; that the means of industry, whatever they may be, left to themselves, always incline themselves to those articles which are the most necessary to nations, and that these necessary articles create at the same time fresh populations, and fresh enjoyments for those populations, all probability is not against me.

Let us go back only two hundred years, and suppose that a merchant had taken a rich cargo to the sites on which the present cities of New York and Philadelphia stand - Would he have sold it? Suppose that, without failing a victim to the natives, he had succeeded in laying the foundation of an agricultural or a manufactural establishment: Would he have sold there any one of his articles? Most certainly not. He would have been obliged to consume them all himself. Why do we see it so different in our days? Why, as soon as goods arrive, or are manufactured at Philadelphia or New York, are we sure to sell them at the course of exchange? It appears evident to me that it is because the farmers, the merchants, and at present the manufacturers, even of New York and Philadelphia, and of the surrounding provinces, produce, and import produce, by the means of which they acquire that which is offered to them by others.

What is true as regards a new State, it will be said is not so of an old one. There was room in America for more producers and more consumers; but in a country where there were already more producers than were necessary, consumers only were wanted. Allow me to answer, that the only real consumers are those who produce on their part, because they alone can buy the produce of others, and that barren consumers can buy nothing except by the means of value created by producers.

It is probable that in the time of the reign of Queen Elizabeth, when England had not half the population of the present day, they had then discovered that there were more laborers than work. I desire no other proof of this than that very law which was then passed in favor of the poor, the result of which is one of the banes of England. Its principal object is to furnish work for the unfortunate who can find no employ. *There was* no employ in a country which since then has been able to furnish enough for a double and triple number of laborers. Whence comes it, Sir, whence comes it, however unfortunate may be the situation of Great Britain? Are more of divers articles sold in it, than in the days of Elizabeth? What can be the cause of this, if not that more is produced? One produces one thing, which he exchanges with his neighbour who produces another. Having more than enough for use, the population is increased, and still everybody has been better supplied.

It is the capability of production which makes the difference between a country and a desert. And the more a country produces, the more it is advanced, the more populous it is, and is the better provided.

This observation, which is self-evident, probably is not denied by you, but you complain of the conclusions I draw from it.

I have asserted that if there is an overstock, a superabundance of many kinds of goods, it is because other goods are not produced in sufficient quantities to be exchanged with the first. That if the producers of them could produce more, or others, the first would find the vent which now fails; in a word, that there is only too much produce of certain kinds because there is not enough of others, and you pretend that there may be a superabundance of all kinds at the same time, citing at the same time facts in your favor. M. de Sismondi had already opposed my doctrine, and I am very glad to quote here his most forcible expressions, in order not to deprive you, Sir, of any advantage that belongs to you, and that my answers may serve for both.

"Europe," says this ingenious author, "is arrived at a point to have, in all its parts, an industry and a manufacture superior to its wants." He adds, that "the incumbrance which results from it begins to be felt in the rest of the world." "Examine the reports of commerce, the newspapers, rand the accounts of travellers, and every where will be seen proofs of that super-abundance of production beyond the consumption, of that manufacture, proportionate, not to the demand, but to the capital employed; of that activity of merchants which induces them to go in crowds to every new settlement, and which exposes them by turns to ruinous losses in every trade in which they expected profit. We have seen merchandise of all kinds, but particularly that of England, the great manufacturing power, abound in all the markets of Italy, in a proportion so far beyond the demand, as to compel the merchants, in order to realise part of their funds, to sell their goods at a loss of a quarter, or a third, instead of at a profit.

The tide of commerce turned away from Italy, found its way into Germany, Russia, and the Brazils, and very soon met with the same obstacles there.

"The last advices inform us of similar losses in new countries. In the month of August, 1818, complaints were made at the Cape of Good Hope, that all the warehouses were filled with European goods, which were offered at a lower price than in Europe, but without finding a sale. In the month of June, at Calcutta, the complaints of commerce were of the same nature. A strange phenomenon at first appeared -- England sending cotton goods to India, and consequently succeeding in working at a lower price than the half-naked inhabitants of Hindostan, and reducing its workmen to a still more miserable state.

"But this whimsical turn giver to commerce did not last long. At present British productions arc cheaper in India than in England itself. In the month of May they were obliged to re-export from New-Holland, European goods which had been sent there in too great abundance. Buenos

Ayres, New Grenada, and Chili, are already returning goods in the same way.

"Mr. Fearon's voyage to the United States, completed only in the spring of 1818, presents this spectacle in a still more striking point of view. From one extremity to the other, of this vast and prosperous continent, there is not a city, nor a town, in which the quantity of goods offered for sale is not infinitely greater than the means of the buyers, notwithstanding the merchants endeavour to induce them, by very long credit, and every kind of facility in the payments, which they take in bills or in provisions of all kinds.

"No fact presents itself to us in a greater number of places, or under more varied shapes, than the disproportion of the means of consumption with the production - than the impossibility which producers find to give up their industry because it is declining, - and the certainty that their ranks are never thinned but by failures. How is it that philosophers will not see that which is evident to every vulgar eye?

"The error into which they have fallen is entirely owing to this false principle - that the production is the same thing as the revenue. Mr. Ricardo, according to M. Say, repeats and affirms it. "M. Say has proved in the most satisfactory manner," says he, "that there is no capital, however large, that cannot be employed, because the demand for produce is only bounded by production." No person produces but with the intention of consuming or selling the article he produces, and no one sells but with the intention of buying some other production, which may be of immediate use, or contribute to future production.

"The producer becomes therefore consumer of his produce, or buyer and consumer of the produce of some other person." "Upon this principle," continues M. de Sismondi, "it becomes absolutely impossible to comprehend or explain the best demonstrated fact in all the history of commerce, viz. the choaking up the markets."[2]

I shall first of all observe, to those persons to whom the facts about which M. de Sismondi afflicts himself with some reason, appear conclusive, that they are in effect conclusive; but that conclusion is against himself.

There are too many English goods offered in Italy and elsewhere, because there are not a sufficient quantity of Italian goods suited to England. A country buys only what it can pay for; for if it did not pay, others would soon cease to sell to it. Now with what do the Italians pay the English? With oil, silks, and raisins; besides these articles and a few others, if they want more English productions, with what would they pay for them? With money! But they must obtain the money wherewith to pay for the English productions. You see clearly, Sir, that in order to obtain productions, a nation, as well as an individual, must have recourse to its own productions.

It is said that the English sell at a loss in those places which they inundate with their goods, which I readily believe. They multiply the goods offered, which depreciates it; and they take specie in payment as much as they can, which consequently makes more scarce and more valuable. Being become more precious, a less quantity is given in each exchange. This is the reason they are obliged to sell at a loss. But suppose for a moment, that the Italians had more capital - that they employed their land and their industrious powers better - in a word, that they produced more; and suppose, at the same time, that the English laws, instead of having been framed upon the absurd idea of the balance of commerce, had admitted, on moderate terms, everything that the Italians could have produced, in payment for English productions; can you imagine that English goods would then incumber the Italian ports, or doubt that a still greater quantity of goods would find a ready sale?

The Brazils, a vast country, highly favored by nature, could consume a hundred times the English goods which accumulate there, and don't sell; but it would be necessary that Brazil should produce all that it is capable of producing; and how is this poor Brazil to succeed in this? All the efforts of her citizens are paralised by her Administration. If any branch of industry appears likely to yield a profit, the executive power seizes and destroys it. If any one finds a precious stone, it is taken away from him. Great encouragement to seek for more wherewith to buy European goods!!

The English Government rejects, on its part, by means of its Custom Houses and Importation Duties, the production which the English might bring from abroad, in exchange for their goods, and even the necessary *provisions*, of which their manufacturers stand so much in need; and this because it is necessary that the English farmers should sell their wheat at above eighty shillings per quarter, in order to enable them to pay the enormous taxes. All these nations complain of the sufferings to which they have reduced themselves by their own fault. This puts me in mind of invalids who are out of temper with their sufferings, but who will not correct themselves of those excesses which are the primary cause of them. I know that an oak is not so easily grubbed up as a pernicious weed. I know that old barriers are not taken away, however rotten they may be, when they are supported by the dirt which has collected around them. I know that certain corrupt and corrupting governments stand in need of monopolies and custom-duties, to pay for the vote of the honorable majorities who pretend to be the representatives of nations. I am not sufficiently unjust to desire that one should govern with a view to the general interest, in order to obtain all the votes without paying for them; but at the same time, why should I be surprised that deplorable consequences should be the result of so many vicious systems?

You will readily admit with me, Sir, at least I presume so, the mischief which nations do to each other by their jealousies, their sordid interest, or by the ignorance of those who set themselves up as their organisers; but you maintain that, even supposing they have had more liberal institutions, the commodities produced may exceed the wants of consumers. Well, Sir, I am ready to defend myself on this ground.

Let us pass over the war which nations carry on against each other with their "*douaniers*," let us consider each people in their relations with themselves, and let us understand, once for all, whether we are beyond the reach of consuming what we are capable of producing.

"M. Say, 'Mr. Mill, and Mr. Ricardo, whom you call the principal authors of the new doctrine of profit, appear to me t.o have fallen into fundamental errors on that subject. In the first place they have looked upon merchandise as though it were an algebraic character instead of being an article of consumption, which must necessarily have reference to the number of consumers, and to the nature of their wants."[3]

I don't know, Sir, at least as far as regards myself, upon what you found that accusation. I have considered this idea in all its shapes -- that the value of things (the only quality which makes them riches) is rounded on their utility, on the aptitude they possess to satisfy our wants.

"The need we have of things, I said,[4] depends upon the moral and physical nature of man, the climate he lives in, and on the manners and legislation of his country. He has wants of the body, wants of the mind, and of the soul; wants for himself, others for his family, others still as a member of society. The skin of a bear, and a reindeer, are articles of the first necessity to a Laplander, whilst the very name of them is unknown to the *Lazzaroni* of Naples. The latter for his part can do without everything, provided he can obtain macaroni. In the stone manner the Courts of Judicature in Europe are considered as one of the strongest bonds of the social body, whilst the indigent people of America, the Arabs, and the Tartars, do very well without them.

"Of these wrests, some are satisfied by the use we make of certain things, with which Nature furnishes us gratuitously, such as the air, water, and the light of the sun. We may call these things *natural riches*, because Nature alone pays the cost of them. As she gives them indiscriminately to all, no one has occasion to acquire them by means of any sacrifice whatever; therefore, they have no exchangeable value.

"Other wants can only be satisfied by the use we make of certain things, to which the use they are of could only, be given them by causing them to undergo a modification, by having effected a change in their state, and by having for that purpose surmounted some difficulty or other. Such are the things which we can only obtain by agricultural process, by commerce, or the arts. These are the only property that has an exchangeable value. The reason of which is evident -- they are, by the simple fact of their production, the result of an exchange in which the producer has given his productive services for the purpose of receiving this produce. From that time they cannot be obtained from him, except by virtue of another exchange -- by giving him another production which he may estimate at as much as his own.

"These things may be called social riches, because no exchange can take place without social intercourse, and because it is only in society that the right of exclusively possessing what has been obtained by production, or exchange, can be guaranteed."

I add; "Let us observe, at the same time, that social riches are, as riches, the only ones which can become the object of a scientific study; 1st. because they are the only ones which are appreciable, or at least whose appreciation is not arbitrary; 2nd. because they are the only ones which are obtained, distributed, and destroyed, agreeably to the laws which we may make."

Is this considering productions as *algebraic characters*, by abstracting the number of consumers, and the nature of their wants? Does not this doctrine establish, on the contrary, that our wants alone compel us to make sacrifices by means whereof we obtain productions?

These sacrifices are the price we pay to obtain them. You call these sacrifices, according to Smith, by the name of labor, which is an insufficient expression, for they include the concurrence of land and capital.

I call them *productive service*. They have every where a price current; as soon as this price exceeds the value of the thing produced, a disadvantageous exchange is the result, in which a greater value has been consumed than has been produced.

As soon as a produce has been created, which is equivalent to services, the services are paid by the produce, the value of which, by being distributed amongst the producers, forms their revenue. You see therefore that this revenue only exists in proportion to the exchangeable value of the produce, and that it can only have that value in consequence of the demand for it, in the present state of society. I do not therefore separate this want, nor do I give it an arbitrary valuation. I take it for what it is -- for what the consumers will have it to be. I could quote, if it were necessary, the whole of my book iii. which details the different modes of consuming, their causes and effects; but 1 will not intrude upon your time and attention. Let, us proceed.

You say "It is by no means true; in fact, that commodities are always bartered for commodities. The greatest part of commodities are directly exchanged for labor, productive or unproductive, and it is evident that this mass of commodities altogether, compared to the labor for which they are to be exchanged, may depreciate in value on account of its superabundance, the same as a single article, in particular, may by its superabundance fall in value in respect to labor or money."[5]

Allow me to observe, in the first place, that I did not say that commodities are always bartered for commodities, but rather that productions are only bought with productions.

In the second place, that those who admit this expression, commodity, might reply to you, that when *commodities* are given in payment of labor, these commodities are in effect exchanged for other commodities, that is to say for those which are produced by the labor that is paid for. But this answer. is not sufficient for those who take a more extended and complete view of the phenomenon of the production of our riches. Allow me to lay before you a striking figure; the public, by whom we are judged, will I hope find great facilities in it, in weighing the merit of your objections and my answers.

For the purpose of showing the operation of industry, capital, and land, in the work of production, I personify them; and I find that each one of these persons sells his services, (which I call *productive services*,) to an enterpriser who is a merchant, a manufacturer, or rather a farmer. This enterpriser having bought the services of a parcel of land, by paying a rent to the proprietor, the services of a capital by paying interest to a capitalist, and the industrious services of laborers, clerks, or agents of any kind, by paying them a salary, consumes and annihilates all these productive services; and from this consumption, a produce of a certain value emanates.

'The value of the produce, provided it be equal to the costs of production, that is to say, to the price which it has been necessary to advance for all the productive services, is sufficient to pay the profits of all those who have contributed, directly or indirectly, to this production

The profit of the enterpriser, on whose account the operation has been made, by deducting the interest of the capital that has been employed, represents the salary for his time and talent, that is to say, his own services productive to himself.

If his capacity was great, and his calculations well made, his profit is considerable. If instead of talent, he has shown ignorance in his business, he will have gained nothing; he will have lost. It is the enterpriser who takes all the risk; but it is he, on the other hand, who benefits by every favorable *result*.

All the productions which daily come before us, and all those which our imaginations tan conceive, have been formed by operations, every one of which forms part of those I have just explained, but combined in an infinity of different ways. What some enterprisers do to obtain certain productions, others do to obtain other productions. Now it is these various productions, which being exchanged against each other, open a reciprocal vent each to the other.. The greater or less want there is of one of these productions, compared with others, determines an exchange at a greater or less price; that is, for a greater or less quantity of any other production. Money is nothing more in this matter than a passing agent, which, the exchange once complete, has nothing more to do with it, but is employed in other exchanges.

It is with the rent of the land, the interest, and the salaries, which form the profits resulting from this production, that the producers purchase the articles of their consumption. Producers are at the same time consumers; and the nature of their wants, having an influence, in different degrees, on the demand for different productions, always favors, when liberty exists, the production of that which is most necessary, because, being the most in demand, it immediately becomes the article which yields the greatest profit to enterprisers.

I have said, that for the purpose of better showing how industry, capital, and land, act in productive operations, I would personify them, and mark the services they render. But this is not a mere fiction: they are facts. Industry is represented by the *industrious* of all classes, capital by the capitalists, and land by the *proprietors*. It is these three classes of persons who sell the productive action of their commodity, and who affix the price to it.

My mode of expressing myself may be censured; but then it will be necessary to produce a better, for it cannot be denied that things take place as I have asserted. I have described the facts. The mode of description may be censured; but don't let anyone flatter himself that he can controvert the facts; there they are, and will defend themselves.

Let us now resume your accusation --You say, Sir, that many commodities are bought with labor; and I go further than you do, I say that they must all be so bought; extending this expression, labor, to the service rendered by capital and land,[6] I say that they cannot be bought in any other way; that it is invariably by such services that use and value are given to things; and that ultimately two things present themselves to us, one of consuming ourselves the utility and consequently the value we have produced, the other to employ it in purchasing the utility and value produced by others; that in both eases we purchase commodities with productive services, and that the greater portion of productive service we employ, the more we can buy.

You pretend that there is no such thing as immaterial produce. Ah! Sir, originally there was no other. A field itself furnished nothing towards the production but its service, which is an immaterial produce. It serves as a crucible in which minerals are put, and from whence tome out metal and dross. Is there any part of the crucible in these productions? No; the crucible serves for a new productive operation. Is there any part of the field in the harvest which it produces? I answer the same: No; for if a fund of land exhausted itself, it would finish at the end of a certain number of years, by being entirely annihilated. A fund of land only returns what is put into it; but this is after an elaboration which I call the *productive service* of the field. I may be criticised about the word, but I fear not any criticism on the subject, because the thing is, and will be, and wherever political economy is studied this will be found to be the fact, whatever name may be thought proper to be given to it. The service which a capital renders, in whatever enterprise it is employed, whether commercial, agricultural, or manufactural, is the same - an *immaterial produce*. He who expends a capital unproductively destroys the capital itself; he who expends it productively expends the material capital, and the service of this capital besides, which is an *immaterial produce*. When a dyer puts one thousand francs' worth of indigo into his cauldron he consumes a thousand francs' worth of indigo, immaterial produce, and he consumes, besides, the time his capital is employed, that is its interest. The dye he obtains returns him the value of the material capital which he has employed, and the value of the immaterial service of this same capital besides.

The service of the workman is also an immaterial produce. The workman leaves his manufactory, in the evening, just as he went into it in the morning. He has left nothing material in his workshop, therefore it is an immaterial service which he has furnished to a productive operation. This service is the daily and annual produce of a fund which I call his *industrious powers*, and which constitutes his wealth; a poor *wealth*! particularly in England, and I know the cause of it.

All these things constitute *immaterial produce*; call. them by whatever name you please, they will be no other than immaterial produce, which will exchange one against the other, or for material produce, and which in all these exchanges will form their regulated price-current, like all other price-currents in the world, on the proportion between the supply and the demand.

All these services, of industry, capital, and land, which are productions independent of all matter, form the *revenue* of all mankind. What! all our revenues are immaterial!! Yes, Sir, all: otherwise it would be necessary that the mass of matter of which the Globe is composed should be augmented every year. This would be necessary in order that every year we might have a fresh material revenue. We neither create nor destroy a single atom. We confine ourselves to changing its combinations, and everything we employ in it is immaterial. It is of value; and it is that value, also immaterial, which we consume daily and yearly, and which keeps us alive; for consumption is a change of form given to matter, or, if you prefer it, a derangement of form, as production is the arrangement of it. If you find anything paradoxical in all these propositions, look at the things they express, and I have no doubt they will appear very simple and very reasonable to you.

Without this analysis I defy you to explain the entire facts; to explain, for example, how the same capital is consumed twice, productively by an enterpriser, and unproductively by his workman. By help of the preceding analysis it will be seen, that the workman supplies his labor, the produce of his capacity, which he sells to the enterpriser -- takes home his salary, which forms his revenue, and consumes it unproductively. The enterpriser, (who has bought the labor of the workman) on his part, by devoting a part of his capital to it, consumes it productively, the same as the dyer productively consumes the indigo he throws into his cauldron. These values, having been reproductively destroyed, reappear in the produce which comes out of the hands of the enterpriser. It is not the enterpriser's capital which forms the workman's revenue, as M. Sismondi pretends. It is in the workshops, and not in the workman's dwelling, that the enterpriser's capital is consumed. The value consumed at the workman's house has another source, it is the produce of his industrious powers. The enterpriser devotes a part of his capital to the purchase of this labor.

Having bought it, he consumes it; and the workman on his part consumes the value he has obtained in exchange for his labor. Wherever there is an exchange, there are two values. created and bartered; and where ever two values are created, there can be and there is in fact two consumptions.[7]

It is the same with productive service yielded by the capital. The capitalist who lends it sells the service, the labor of his commodity, and the daily or yearly price, which an enterpriser pays him for it, is called interest. The two terms of exchange are, the one service ate capital, the other interest.

The enterpriser, at the same time that he productively consumes the capital, also productively consumes the service of the capital. The lender, on his part, who has sold the service of his capital, unproductively consumes the interest of it, which is a material value, given in exchange for the immaterial service of the capital. It is astonishing that there is a double consumption: that of the enterpriser to make his produce, and that of the capitalist to satisfy his wants, since there are the two terms of one exchange, two values proceeding from two different funds, bartered, and both consumable?

You say, Sir, that the distinction between productive and unproductive labor is the earner stone of *Adam Smith's* work, and that to call, as I have done, that labor productive which is not fixed in any material object, is to overthrow his work from top to bottom. No, Sir, this is not the earner stone of Adam Smith's work, since, that stone being shaken, the edifice is imperfect without being less stable. What will eternally support that excellent work is, that it proclaims in all its pages, that the *changeable value* of things is the foundation of all wealth. It is from that time that political economy is become a positive science; for the price-current of each thing is a determined quantity, the elements of which may be analised, the causes assigned, the bearings studied, and the changes foreseen. By taking away from the definition of wealth this essential character, allow me to inform you, Sir, we replunge the science into the surge, and drive it back.

Far from undermining the celebrated inquiries into the Wealth of Nations, I support them in all their essential parts; but at the stone time, I think Adam Smith has misconceived real exchangeable value, by forgetting that which is attached to productive service, which leaves no trace behind, because the whole of it is consumed. I think he has also forgotten real services, which even leave traces behind them, in material productions such as service of capital, consumed, independently of the capital itself. I think he has got into infinite obscurity, for want of having distinguished the consumption of the industrious services of an enterpriser, from the services of his capital -- a distinction so real, however, that there is scarcely any commercial house that does not keep these accounts under distinct heads.

I revere Adam Smith, -- he is my master. At the commencement of my career in Political Economy, whilst yet tottering, and driven on the one hand by the Doctors of the Balance of Trade, and on the other by the Doctors of Net Proceeds, I stumbled at every step, he showed me the right road. Leaning upon his *Wealth of Nations*, which at the same time discovers to us the wealth of his genius, I learned to go alone. Now I no longer belong to any school, and shall not share the ridicule of the Reverend Jesuit Fathers who translated *Newton's* Elements, with notes. They felt that the laws of natural philosophy did not well accord with those of Loyola; they also took care to inform the public by an Advertisement, that although they had apparently shown the motion of the Earth, in order to complete the development of celestial philosophy, they were not less under subjection to the decrees of the Pope, who did not admit this motion. I am only under the subjection of the decrees of eternal Reason, and I am not afraid to say so. *Adam Smith* has not embraced the whole of the phenomenon of the production and consumption of wealth, but he has done so much that we ought to feel grateful to him. Thanks to him, the most vague, the most obscure of sciences will soon become the most precise, and that which of all others will leave the fewest points unexplained.

Let us figure to ourselves, producers (and under this name I comprise as well the possessors of capitals and lands, as the possessors of industrious powers,) let us fancy them advancing, to meet each other with their productive services, or the profit which has resulted from them (an immaterial quality). This profit is their produce. Sometimes it is fixed on an immaterial object, which is transmitted with the immaterial produce, but which in itself is of no importance, is nothing, in political Economy: for matter, dispossessed of value, is not wealth. Sometimes it is transmitted, is sold by one, and bought by another, without being fixed in any matter. It is the advice of the Doctor or the Lawyer, the service of the Soldier or the public Officer. Every one exchanges the utility he produces against that which is produced by others, and in every one of these exchanges, which are carried to account in a book of competition, as the utility offered by *Paul* is more or less in demand than that offered by *Jacques*, it sells dearer or cheaper -- that is to say, that it obtains in exchange more or less of the utility offered by the latter. It is in this sense that the influence of the demand and supply must be understood.[8]

This, Sir, is not a doctrine advanced by way of afterthought; it is to be found in sundry parts of my *Treatise on Political Economy*;[9] and by the help of my Epitome its coincidence with every other principle of the science, and with all the facts which serve for its basis, is fundamentally the same. It is already professed in many parts of Europe; but I earnestly desire that it may succeed in convincing you, and that it may appear to you to be worthy of being introduced into the chair, which you fill with so much eclat.

After these necessary explanations, you will not accuse me of finesse if I rest upon those laws which I have shown to be rounded on the nature of things and on the facts which issue from them.

Commodities, you say, are only exchanged for commodities: they are also exchanged for labor. If this labor be a produce that some persons sell, that others buy, and that the latter consume, it will cost me very little to call it a *Commodity*, and it will cost vou very little more to assimilate other commodities to it, for they are also produce.. Then comprising both under the generic name of *Produce*, you may perhaps admit that produce is bought only with produce.

LETTER THE SECOND.

SIR,

I think I have proved in my first letter that Produce can only be bought with Produce. I still see no cause to abandon this doctrine, that it is production which opens a market for production. It is true that I have taken as produce, all the services which proceed from our personal capacities, from our capitals, and our property in land, which has put me under the necessity of sketching afresh, and in other terms, the Doctrine of Production, which Smith evidently has neither understood, nor entirely described.

However, Sir, on reading again the 3rd section of your chapter 7,[10] I feel that there is still one point in which you do not agree with me. You will perhaps confess that produce is bought only with other produce, but you persist in maintaining that men can, putting all productions together, produce a quantity more than equal to their wants, and consequently -- thief there will be no employ for a part of these productions -- that there may be a superabundance and glut of all kinds at the same time. For the purpose of presenting your objection in all its force, I will transform it into a figure, and will say, M. Malthus readily admits that one hundred sacks of wheat will purchase a hundred pieces of cloth, in a partnership which has occasion for this quantity of cloth and wheat to clothe and feed themselves, but that if the same company should produce two hundred sacks of wheat and two hundred pieces of cloth, it would be in vain that these two commodities could be exchanged the one for the other: he will maintain that a part of them woukl find no buyers. I must therefore, Sir, prove in the first place, that whatever be the quantity produced, and the consequent depreciation of its price, a quantity produced of one kind is always sufficient to enable the producer to acquire the quantity produced of another kind; and after having proved that the possibility of acquiring exists, I must enquire how those productions which superabound give rise to wants to consume them.

The farmer who produces wheat, after having bought the productive services of the land, of the capital he employs, and of his servants, and having added his own labour to it, has consumed all these values to convert them into sacks of wheat, and each sack, including his own labour, that is to say his profit, we will suppose returns him 30 francs. On the other hand the manufacturer who produces flaxen, woollen, or cotton cloth, no matter which, -- the manufacturer in fact after having in the same manner consumed the services of his capital, his own services, and those of his men, has manufactured pieces of cloth, each of which also returns him 30 francs. If you will allow me to come at once to the main point of the question, I will confess to you that my cloth-merchant represents in my mind the producers of all manufactured produce, and my wheat-merchant the producers of all the provisions of life and raw materials. The question is, whether the whole of their two productions, to whatever extent they may be multiplied, and whatever may be the consequent depression in their price, can be bought by their producers, who are at the same time their consumers, and how the want continually increases in proportion to the quantity produced.

We will first examine what takes place in the hypothesis of a perfect liberty, which allows the indefinite multiplication of all productions, and afterwards we will examine into the obstacles which the nature of things or the imperfections of society oppose to this indefinite liberty of production. But you will say that the hypothesis of an indefinite production is more favorable to your cause, because it is more difficult to dispose of an unlimited than of a circumscribed production, and that the hypothesis of a circumscribed production, sometimes from one cause sometimes another, is more favorable to mine, which establishes, that it is these very restrictions which, by preventing certain productions, injure the purchase that might be made of those productions which can only be indefinitely multiplied.

In the hypothesis of perfect liberty, the producer of wheat arrives at market with a sack which yields him, including his profit, 30 francs; and the producer of cloth with a piece which brings him the same price: and consequently with two productions which exchange equally:[11] that which sells above its cost of production, will induce a part of the producers of the other commodity to turn to the production of this until the productive services are equally paid by both. This is an effect generally admitted.

It is right to observe that in this hypothesis the producers of the piece of cloth altogether have gained sufficient to buy in the whole piece or any other production of equal value. - - If it amounts for example to 30 francs, including everything even the manufacturer's profit at the rate at which competition has fixed it, this sum is found distributed amongst the producers of the piece of cloth, but in unequal parts, according to the kind and quantity of services rendered to produce it.

If the piece contains ten ells, he who has gained 6 francs can buy two ells of it, he who has gained 30 sons can only buy half an ell, but it is still clear that all of them together can buy the whole piece. That, if instead of buying cloth they wish to buy wheat, they can also buy the whole quantity, because like the cloth it is only worth 30 francs, the same as they can buy indifferently according to their wants, either a portion of the piece of cloth or an equivalent part of the sack of wheat.

He who has gained by either of these productions six francs, may employ three francs in a tenth of the piece of cloth, and three francs in a tenth of the wheat, still it is true that all the producers together can acquire the. whole of the productions.

It is here, Sir, that you ground your objections.-- If productions increase, you say, or wants diminish, the productions will fall to too low a price to pay for the labour necessary to their production.[12] Before I reply to you, Sir, I inform you that, if out of politeness I make use of your word labour, which, according to the explanation given in my preceding letter, is incomplete,

I shall comprise under that term, not only the productive service of a workman and his master, but also the productive services rendered by the capital and the land, services which have their 'price, as well as personal labor, and so real a price that the capitalist and the landholder live upon it.

This point being understood, I reply, in the first place, that productions by diminishing in price do not disenable the producers to purchase the labor which has created them, or any other equivalent labor. In our hypothesis the producers of corn, by a more skilful process, will produce a double quantity of corn, and the producers of cloth a double quantity of cloth, and the corn as well as the cloth will be diminished one half, in price. What does this mean? The producers of corn will have two sacks for their services, which together will be worth what a single sack was worth, and the producers of cloth will have two pieces, which together will be worth what one was worth. In the exchange called *production* the same services will have obtained, each in their place, a double quantity of production, but these two double quantities may be obtained one by the other as heretofore, and as easily so, that without laying out more in productive services, a nation in which this productive power begins to unfold itself, will have double the quantity of articles to consume, either wheat, or cloth, or anything else, since we have agreed to represent by wheat and cloth everything the human species may want for its support. The productions in such an exchange are opposed in value to productive services. Now, as in every exchange one of the two articles is of greater value, in proportion to the quantity it obtains of the other, it follows, that productive services are the more valuable in proportion as productions are multiplied, and at lower price.[13]

This is the reason why the diminution in the price of productions, by augmenting the value of the productive funds of a nation, and the revenues resulting therefrom, increases the national wealth. This demonstration, which is detailed in the 3rd Chapter of the 2d. Book of my Treatise on Political Economy (4th edition), has I think rendered some service to the science by explaining that which up to that period had been felt but not explained. Which is, that although wealth is a changeable value, general wealth has accrued by the low price of commodities and every kind of production.[14]

Never perhaps has an increase of double in the productive power of labor taken place all at once, and in all productions at the same time, but it is indisputable that it has taken place gradually in many productions, and in very varied proportions. A purple cloak amongst the ancients, of the same quality and size, of the same solidity and beauty of color, cost no doubt double what it costs now. And I have no doubt that wheat, paid in labor, is diminished one half at least since the unknown epochs of the invention of the plough. All these productions costing less labor, have been, in consequence of competition, given for what they cost, without any one being a loser by it, and all the world has gained in revenue.

But we must return to the first part of your objection. *The producers of wheat and the producers of cloth will then produce more wheat and cloth than either the one or the other can consume.* Ah! Sir, after having proved that notwithstanding a reduction of more than half the value of the productions the same labor could buy the whole of them, and thereby procure double the means of existence and enjoyment, shall I be reduced to the necessity of proving to the justly celebrated author of the *Essay on Population* that everything that can be produced may find consumers, and that amongst the enjoyments which the quantity of productions of which mankind can dispose, procure, the comforts of home and the increase of children are not the least? After having written three justly admired volumes to prove that the population always rises to the level of the means of existence, can you admit the case *of a great increase of productions, with a stationary number of consumers, and wants reduced by parsimony*? (page 355.)

Either the Author of the *Essay on Population or the author of the Principles of Political Economy* must be wrong. But everything proves to us that it is not the author of the *Essay on Population* who is wrong. Experience as well as reason shows that a production, a *thing necessary or agreeable* to man, is only despised when one has not the means of buying it. These means of buying it are precisely what establish the demand for the production, which set a price to it. Not to want a useful thing is not to have wherewith to pay for it. And how is it we have not wherewith to pay for it? It is because we are deprived of that which constitutes wealth, deprived of either industry, land, or capital.

When men are once provided with the means of producing, they appropriate their productions to their wants, for the production itself is an exchange in which the productive means are supplied, and in which the article we most want is demanded in return. To create a thing, the want of which does not exist, is to create a thing without value: this would not be production. Now from the moment it has a value, the producer can find means to exchange it for those articles he wants.

This power of exchange, peculiar to man amongst all the animals, appropriates all productions to all wants, and allows him to calculate for his existence not on the species of production (he will exchange it as soon as he likes if it has a value but on the value.

The difficulty, you will say, is to create articles which are worth the expences of their production; in my next letter you will see what I think on this subject. But in the hypothesis in which we still are, of the liberty of industry, you will allow me to observe that there is no difficulty experienced in creating articles which are worth the expences of their production, except the high demands of suppliers of productive services. Now the high price of productive services denotes that what we seek for exists, that is to say, that there is a mode of employing them so as to make the produce sufficient to repay what they cost.

You reproach those who subscribe to my opinion with "having no regard to the influence so general and so important of man's disposition to indolence and laziness" (page 358). You suppose a case, in which men after having produced wherewith to satisfy their most necessary wants would prefer to do nothing more, the love of ease being predominant in their minds over that of pleasure. This supposition, allow me to say, proves in my favor and against you. What more shall I say than that we only sell to those who produce? Why are not articles of luxury sold to a farmer who likes to lead a rustic life? Because he had rather be idle than produce wherewith to purchase them. Whatever be the cause that circumscribes production, whether the want of capital, of population, of diligence, or liberty, the effect in my mind is the same: the articles which are offered on the one hand are not sold because too few are produced on the other.

You look upon indolence that will not produce as directly against a vent, and I am entirely of your opinion. But then, how can you consider as you do (ch. 7 sec. 9) the indolence of what you call unproductive consumers as favorable to this same vent. It is absolutely necessary you say (page 463) that a country which has great means of production should posses a numerous body of unproductive consumers. How can it be that that indolence which refuses to produce, should overate against a vent in the first ease, and be favorable to it in the second.

If I must speak plain, this indolence is against it in both eases. Who do you mean by this numerous body of unproductive consumers so necessary in your opinion to producers? Are they the proprietors of land and capitals? Doubtless they do not produce directly, but their property produces for them. They consume the value, to the creation of which their lands and capitals have contributed. They contribute therefore to the production, and can only purchase what they do, in consequence of that contribution. If they further contribute by their labor, and join to their profit as proprietors and capitalists other profit as laborers, thereby producing more, they can consume more, but it is not in their character of non-producers that they augment the vent of producers.

Do you mean public functionaries, soldiers, and state pensioners? Neither is it in their character of non-producers that they favor a vent. I am far from contesting the legitimacy of the emoluments they receive, but I cannot think that those who pay taxes would be at a loss what to do with their money if the collector did not come to their assistance either their wants would be more amply satisfied, or they would employ the same money in a reproductive manner. In either ease, the money would be spent and would favor the vent of some productions equal in value to what is now purchased by those you call unproductive consumers. Confess therefore, Sir, that it is not by unproductive consumers that the vent is favored, but rather by those who help to keep them, and that in ease the unproductive consumers should happen to disappear, which God forbid, the vent would not be injured the value of a single halfpenny.

I know no better on what principle you decide (page 856) that production cannot go on if the value of commodities only pays a little more than the labor they have cost. It is by no means necessary that the produce should yield more than the cost of production, to enable the producers to go on. When an enterprise begins with a capital of a hundred thousand francs, it is sufficient if it yield a produce or a hundred thousand francs, to enable it to recommence its operation. And where, you ask, are the producer's profits? The whole capital has served to pay them.[15] And it is the price that has been paid for it which forms the revenue of all the producers. If the produce resulting from it is worth only a hundred thousand francs, the same capital is re-established and all the producers are paid.[16]

I am therefore not afraid of making your objection stronger than you have done by expressing it thus: "Although each commodity may have cost in its production the same quantity of labor and capital, and the one may be equivalent to the other, still they may both be so abundant, as not to purchase more labor than they cost. In this case, can production go on? certainly not." No? why not, I beseech you? Why cannot the farmers and manufacturers, who make together 60 francs worth of wheat and cloth, who I have shown would be in a situation to purchase this entire quantity of commodity, sufficient for their wants, why can they not after having bought and consumed it, begin again? They would have the same land, the same capital, the stone industry as before, they would be precisely where they were when they began, and they would have lived, and supported themselves upon their income from the sale of their productive services. What more is necessary for the preservation of society? This great phenomenon Production being analysed and shewn in its true colors explains everything.

After the apprehension you are under, Sir, that the productions of society should outstep in quantity what it can and will consume, it is natural you should behold these capitals increased by parsimony, with terror, for the capitals which seek employment, occasion an increase of production and fresh means of accumulation, from whence arise productions: in fact you seem to me to be afraid that we shall be stifled under a mass of wealth, which fear I confess to you by no means troubles me.

Was it for you, Sir, to stir up popular prejudices against those who do not spend their income in articles of luxury? You admit (page 351) *that no permanent increase of wealth can take place without a previous augmentation of capital*! you admit (page 352) that those who work are consumers as well as those who are idle, and still you fear that if we are always accumulating *we cannot consume the quantity (continually increasing) of commodities produced by these new laborers*. (page 353.)

Your vain fears must be destroyed, but first of all allow me to make a reflexion on the object of modern Political Economy, of a nature to direct us in our course.

What is it that distinguishes us from the Economists of the school of Quesnay? It is the pains we take to observe the connexion of the facts which regard wealth, the rigorous exactitude we impose upon ourselves in the description of them. Now to comprehend well, and describe well, we must as much as possible remain passive spectators. Not that we cannot nor ought sometimes to sigh at those gross operations, of the unhappy consequences of which we are often the sorrowful and helpless witnesses. Is the philanthropic historian interdicted from those sorrowful reflexions which the iniquities of policy sometimes draw from him? But a reproach, a thought, an advice are not history, and I am bold to say, are not Political Economy. What we owe to the public is to tell them how and why such a fact is the consequence of such other fact; whether they court or dread the consequence, that is sufficient for them, they know what they have to do, but no exhortations.

It consequently appears to me that I ought no more to preach, saving after the example of Adam Smith, than you ought to cry up dissipation after that of my Lord Lauderdale. Let us therefore confine ourselves to the observing how things follow and are linked together in the accumulation of capital.

In the first place I remark the major part of accumulations are necessarily slow. All the world, whatever income they may have, must live before they accumulate, and what I here call life is in general more expensive in proportion as we are rich. In most trades and professions, the maintenance and establishment of a family require the whole of the income and oftentimes the capital, and although something yearly may be saved, it is generally very disproportionate to the capital actually employed. An enterpriser who has a hundred thousand francs and industry, gains in ordinary eases and in a moderate time from twelve to fifteen thousand francs. Now with such a capital, and industry which is worth as much, that is to say a fortune of two hundred thousand francs, he is economical if he spends only ten thousand, in which ease he would only save yearly five thousand francs or the twentieth part of his capital.

If you divide this fortune as is often the ease between persons, one of whom furnishes the industry, the other the capital, the saving is then much less, because in that ease two families instead of one have to be maintained from the united profits of the capital and industry.[17] At all events it is only very great fortunes that can make great savings, and very large fortunes are rare in all countries. Capitals cannot therefore increase with a rapidity capable of producing the overthrow of industry.

I cannot subscribe to the fears which make you express, in page 357, "That a country is always more exposed to the rapid increase of the funds destined for the support of the laboring class than of the laboring class itself." Nor am I frightened at the enormous increase of production which may result from an augmentation (so slow in its nature) of capital. I see on the contrary these new capitals and the incomes they produce distribute themselves in the most favorable manner amongst producers. In the first place the capitalist in augmenting his capital sees his income increase, which induces greater enjoyments. A capital increased one year buys the following year a little more industrious service. These services being more in demand are paid a little better. A greater number of industrious persons find employ and the reward of their faculties. They work and unproductively consume the produce of their labor, so that if there are more productions created in consequence of this increase of capital there are also more productions consumed. Now what is this but an increase of prosperity?

You say (pages 352 and 360) that if the savings have no other object than the increase of capital, "if the capitalists do not increase their enjoyments with their income, they have not a sufficient motive for saving: for men do not save for a philanthropy's sake, and merely to make industry prosper." That is true. But what conclusion will you draw from it? If they save, I say they encourage industry and production, and this increase of production distributes itself in a manner very advantageous to the public. If they do not save I know not what to say. But you cannot conclude from that, that producers will be benefitted by it, for what the capitalists would have saved, would still have been spent. By spending it unproductively, the expenditure is not made greater. As to sums accumulated without being productively consumed, for instance, those hoarded up in the miser's coffer, neither *Smith*, myself, nor any one undertakes to defend this, but they alarm us but little in the first place, because they are very inconsiderable in comparison to the productive capitals of a Nation, and in the second place because their consumption is no more than suspended. There are no treasures that have not some time or other been spent either productively or unproductively.

I do not know upon what principle you consider reproductive expences, such as for digging canals, agricultural buildings, constructing machines, and paying artists and artisans, as more favorable to producers than improductive expenses such as those which are only for the personal gratification of the prodigal. "So long," you say (page 363,) "as cultivators are disposed to consume the articles of luxury created by the manufacturers, and the manufacturers the articles of luxury created by the cultivators, all is well. But if either class were disposed to economise with a view of bettering their condition and of providing for the establishment of their families, the case would be quite different," (that is to say apparently, that everything would go ill).

"The farmer instead of allowing his wife ribbons, laces, and velvets, would be content with plainer clothing for her, but his economy would take away from the manufacturer the power of purchasing so great a quantity of his produce, and he would no longer find a vent for the produce of land upon which nothing had been spared in labor and amendment. If the manufacturer on his part instead of gratifying his desires by the consumption of sugar, plumbs, and tobacco, wishes to lay up for the future, he cannot succeed, thanks to the parsimony of the farmer, and to the want of demand for the productions of manufacture.

And a little further on (page 365) "The population necessary to furnish clothing for such a society by the help of machines would be reduced to a trifling number, and would absorb but a small part of the excess of a rich and well cultivated territory. There would evidently be a general falling off in the demand, either for productions or population. And whilst it is certain that a proper passion for consumption (unproductive) would preserve a just proportion between the supply and demand, whatever may be the power of production, it: does not appear less clear that an inclination to save must inevitably lead to a production of commodities exceeding what the organisation and habits of such a society would permit them to consume."

You go so far as to ask what would become of the commodities, if every kind of consumption, bread and water excepted, were suspended only for six months[18] and, it is to me in the first instance that you address this question.

In this and the preceding passage you implicitly rest upon the fact, that a produce saved is withdrawn from every kind of consumption, whilst in all the discussions in all the works you attack, in those of Adam Smith, Mr. Ricardo, mine, and even your own,[19] it is established that a produce saved is a value withdrawn from an unproductive consumption to add it to the capital, that is, to that value which we consume, or cause to be consumed reproductively. *What would become of the commodities, if every kind, of consumption, bread and water excepted, were suspended for six months*? why, Sir, they would sell for the stone amount, for at length what would thereby be added to the amount of the capitals would buy meat, beer, clothes, shirts, shoes and furniture for that class of producers which the sums saved would set to work. *But if we lived on bread and water and did not employ our savings? That is, you suppose we should impose upon ourselves generally an extravagant fast for pleasure and without an object.*

What answer, Sir, would you give to him who amongst the number of strange events which may happen in society, should include the ease of the moon's falling upon the earth. An ease not physically impossible. Her rencontre with a suspended comet, or the-mere stoppage of this star in its orbit would be sufficient. Nevertheless I suspect you will think this question rather impertinent, and I confess to you that you will not be altogether wrong.

I admit that this is a method which philosophy does not disown, to push principles to the greatest possible extremity for the purpose of exaggerating them and discovering their errors, but this exaggeration itself is an error when the nature of things alone presents obstacles continually increasing to the excess we imagine, thereby rendering the supposition inadmissible. You oppose to all those who think with *Adam Smith* that saving is a good, the inconvenience of an excessive saving; but here the excess carries its remedy along with it. Where the capitals become too abundant, the interest which the capitalists derive from them become too low to balance the privations they impose upon themselves by their savings. Safe employment for capital will be difficult to be found; capitals are employed abroad. The common course of nature puts a stop to many accumulations. A great part of those which take place in families in easy circumstances, cease the moment it becomes necessary to provide for the settlement of the children. The income of the fathers, being reduced by this circumstance, they lose the means of accumulation, at the same time that they lose a part of the motives they had for accumulating. Many savings are stopped by death. A property is divided between heirs, and legatees, whose situation in no way resembles that of the deceased, and who frequently dissipate a part of the property instead of increasing it; that part which goes to government is most undoubtedly dissipated, for the state does not employ it reproductively.

The prodigality and ignorance of many persons who lose a part of their capital in ill-conceived enterprizes must necessarily be set against the savings of many others. Every thing serves to convince us that in what relates to accumulations as well as all the rest there is much less danger in letting things take their natural course than to endeavour to give them a forced direction.

You say (page 495) that in certain cases it is contrary to the principles of a sound Political Economy, to recommend saving. Ah Sir! A good Political Economy recommends little, it shews what a capital judiciously employed adds to the power of industry, the same as a good agriculture teaches what irrigation well directed adds to the power of the soil; for the rest it gives to mankind the truths it unfolds, it is for them to make use of them according to their intelligence and capacity.

All that is required, Sir, of so enlightened a man as yourself, is not to propagate the popular error, that prodigality any more than saving is beneficial to producers.[20]

We are too much inclined to sacrifice the future for the present. The principle of every amendment is on the contrary the sacrifice of the temptations of the moment for the future good. This is the ground-work of all virtue, and of all wealth. The man who loses his reputation by violating a deposit, he who ruins his health because he will not resist his inclinations, and he who spends to-day his means of getting to-morrow, all equally fail in economy, and this is what has given rise to the saying that vice is after all nothing more than a bad calculation.

How is it Mr. Malthus does not see that marriage produces children and consequently fresh wants, whilst capitals have no wants, but on the contrary carry with them the means of satisfying them?

LETTER THE THIRD.

SIR,

We have been arguing upon the hypothesis of an indefinite liberty given to a nation, to carry to as great an extent as possible every kind of production, and I think I have proved that if this hypothesis were to be realised, that nation would be able to purchase whatever it chose. From this power, and man's natural desire, continually to better his condition, would infallibly proceed an infinite multiplication of individuals and enjoyments.

This is not however the ease. Nature on the one hand, and the vices of social community on the other, have set bounds to this indefinite power of production, and the enquiry into these obstacles, by bringing us into the real world will serve to prove, in addition to the doctrine established in my treatise on Political Economy, that it is these obstacles to production which alone prevent the circulation and the vent of productions.

I do not pretend to be able to point out all the obstacles which counteract production. Many of them will no doubt be discovered as Political Economy improves, others will perhaps never be discovered, but very powerful ones may be already descried both in natural and political order.

In natural order, the production of alimentary provisions has closer bounds prescribed to it than the production of provisions of furniture and clothes. At the same time, that mankind has need either in weight or value, of a greater quantity of alimentary produce, than of all the rest put together, these productions cannot be brought from a great distance, for their transmittal is difficult, and keeping them is expensive. As to those which can be grown within the territory of a nation, they have their limits, which a more perfect system of agriculture, and larger capitals engaged in agricultural operations, can no doubt remove,[21] but which must exist somewhere. *Arthur Young* thinks France scarcely produces half the alimentary provisions, she is capable of producing.[22] Suppose *Arthur Young says* true. Suppose even that with a better system of agriculture, France should grow twice the quantity of rural produce, without having more agriculturists,[23] she would then have 45 million inhabitants who could employ themselves in any other occupation than agriculture. Her manufactural productions would find greater vent in the country than they do at present, and the surplus would find a vent among the manufacturing population itself. We should not be worse fed than we are now, but in general we should be better provided with manufactured articles; we should have better habitations, better furniture, finer clothes, and articles of use, instruction, and amusement, which are now attainable by a. very small number of persons. All the rest of the population is still rude and uncultivated.

Still, in proportion as the manufacturing class increased, alimentary provisions would become more in demand, and dearer, in comparison with manufactured articles. The latter would procure more restricted profits and salaries, which would discourage their production; and thus it may be conceived, how those bounds which Nature sets to agricultural productions, would also set them to manufactural productions. But this effect, like every thin~ which happens naturally and arises out of the nature of things, is a long way in the perspective, and would be accompanied with less inconvenience than any other possible event.

In admitting these bounds -- set by Nature herself, to the production of food, and indirectly to that of all other articles -- it may be asked, how very industrious countries, such as England, in which capitals abound, and communication is easy, are obstructed in the circulation of their commodities, long before their agricultural productions are arrived at a height beyond which they cannot go. There is then a vice, a hidden evil which torments them. There are probably more, and these will discover themselves successively; but already I perceive one, immense and disastrous, worthy of the most serious attention.

If it should happen that, after every commercial, manufactural, or agricultural enterprise, a man, a collector of duties, should come and establish himself; and that this man, without adding any thing to the merit of the production, to its usefulness, or to that quality which makes it sought. after and sells it, should nevertheless add to the cost of its production; what would be the result of this, I ask you? The price that is set upon an article, even when one has the means of attaining it,[24] depends on the enjoyment we expect from it, or the use it may be of. In proportion as the price gets up, it ceases, with respect to many persons, to be worth what it costs, and the number of its buyers decreases.

Besides, the tax not increasing the profit of any producer, but still enhancing the price of every article, the producer's income is no longer adequate to the purchase of the productions, from the moment that an accident such as I have just mentioned augments their price.

Let us explain to ourselves this effect by number, in order to trace it to its ultimate consequences. It is worth the pains bestowed upon it, if it points out to us the principal cause of an evil that threatens every industrious nation on the face of the earth. England already by her sufferings, warns other nations of the calamities in reserve for them; which will be the more disastrous, in proportion as a robust constitution induces them, more or jess, to very great exertions, from which very beneficial effects will result if not circumscribed, and frightful convulsions if they are.

If the enterpriser, the producer of a piece of cloth, at the same time that he divides between himself and his brother producers a sum of 30 francs, for the productive services which have been employed in the manufacture of the cloth, is obliged to pay besides 6 francs to the tax-gatherer, either he must cease to manufacture cloth, or must sell his piece for 36 francs.[25] But the piece being at 36 francs, the producers, who altogether have only received 30 for it, can only purchase five-sixths of that same piece which previously they could purchase entirely, he who bought an ell of it could now only buy five-sixths of an ell, and so of the rest.

The producer of wheat, who on his part pays to another tax-gatherer a contribution of 6 francs for a sack which cost 30 francs in productive services, is obliged to sell his sack for 36 francs instead of thirty. The consequence of which is, that the producers of wheat and the producers of cloth, whether they want wheat or cloth, can only, with the profit they have made, purchase five-sixths of their productions.

This effect taking place in two reciprocal productions, may take place generally in all productions. -- Without changing the position of the question, we may suppose that the producers, to whatever production they have devoted themselves, have occasion successively for drink, autumnal provisions, lodging, amusements, and articles of luxury or necessity. And still they will find these productions dearer than they can afford, whatever their income may be, according to the rank they hold among producers. There will always be, in the hypothesis which serves as our example, a sixth of the productions remaining unsold.

It is true, that the 6 francs levied by the collector go to somebody, and that those whom the collector represents, (public functionaries, military men, or state pensioners,) may employ this money in the purchase of the remaining sixth, either of the wheat or cloth or of any other production. -- This is indeed the fact; but observe that consumption takes place at the expense of the producers, and that the collector, or his constituents, if they consume a sixth of the productions, thereby compel the producers to feed and clothe themselves -- in fact to live upon five-sixths of what they produce.

This will be admitted; but at the same time it will be said, that it is possible for everyone to live upon five-sixths of what he produces.-- I will admit it myself if it is wished; but I shall ask in my turn, if you think the producer would live as well if two-sixths or a third, instead of one-sixth, were taken from him. No -- but he would still live. Ah! you think he would live! In this case, I ask if he would still live if two-thirds -- three-quarters -- were taken from him; but I perceive that no answer is given.

Now, Sir, I flatter myself that my answer to your most forcible objections will be easily understood, as well as my answer to those of M. Sismondi. If, you say, it is sufficient to create fresh productions, in order to be enabled to consume or exchange them for those which superabound, and thereby procure a vent for both the one and the other, why are they not created? Are the capitals wanting? They abound; enterprises are sought for, in which to employ them to advantage: it is evident they are not to be found you say (page 499); that every kind of commerce is so overloaded with capitals and laborers, both of which offer their productions at a reduced price says M. Sismondi.[26]

I do not mean to say, that it is the act of a dupe, to devote oneself to the useful arts; but you must admit, gentlemen, that if it should ever become so, the effect would be no other than that of which you complain. In order to buy those productions which superabound, it would be necessary to create other productions; but if the situation of producers was too disadvantageous; if after having used means of production sufficient to produce a bullock, a sheep only was the result; if only the same portion of utility as is found in a sheep could be obtained in exchange against any other produce, who would produce at such a disadvantage? Those who had devoted themselves to production, would have made a bad bargain; they would have made an advance which the utility of their production is not sufficient to repay. Whoever should be ~so unwise as to create a production capable of purchasing the former, would have to struggle against the same disadvantages, and would get into the same embarrassment. The profit he would obtain from his production would not indemnify him for his expences; and what he could purchase with this production would be worth no more. Then the workman could no longer live by his labor, and would become a burthen to his parish.[27] Then the enterpriser, no longer enabled to live upon his profits, would renounce his industry. He would purchase stock, or rather go abroad to seek better fortune, a more lucrative occupation, or what comes exactly to the same thing, a production which should be accompanied with less expences.[28] If he should there meet with other inconveniences, he would still seek another scene for his talents, and different countries would be seen driving away, seizing by the head, both their capitals and laborers; that is to say, what is sufficient to carry the prosperity of human societies to the highest pitch, when they know their real interest and the means of benefiting by it.

I shall not take upon myself to say which of the features of this picture are suitable to your country, or to any other, but I leave them to your examination, and to that of all honest men, of good intentions, and who desire to found their happiness on the interesting, laborious, and useful part of mankind.

Why do the savages of the new world, whose precarious subsistence depends upon the chance of the chase, refuse to build villages, and enclose and cultivate land? It is because this sort of life requires too assiduous and too painful a labor. They are wrong; bad calculators, for the privations they endure are much worse than the shackles of a well understood social life would impose upon them. But if this social life were a galley, in which by rowing with all their might for sixteen hours out of the twenty-four, they only obtained a morsel of bread insufficient for their support; they would then indeed be excusable for not preferring a social life. Now everything which renders the situation of a producer -- of a man essential to society -- worse, tends to destroy the principle of existence of the social body, to approximate a civilised people to barbarians, to bring on an order of things in which less is produced and less consumed, to destroy civilisation, which is more flourishing in proportion as more is produced and more consumed. You remark in many places, that man is naturally indolent; and it is to know him but little "to suppose that he would always consume all that he is capable of producing, (page 503)". Indeed you are right; nor do I hold a different opinion when I say that the utility of productions is no longer worth the productive services at the price one is obliged to pay for them.

You yourself seem to have admitted this truth, when you said in another place, (page 842,) "a tax may put an end to the production of a commodity, if no person can consent to put upon this commodity a price equivalent to the fresh difficulties of its production." And this internal vice, {to have cost more in producing than the. thing is worth), is transmitted with the commodity to the end of the world. -- It is everywhere too dear to be worth what it cost, because everywhere we are obliged to pay for it by productive services equal to those it has cost.

A consideration which is not to be despised either, is that the costs of production are not only increased by the multiplied taxes, and by the high price of every thins, but also by the customs which are the result of a vicious political system. If the progress of luxury and large emoluments; the facility of obtaining illegitimate profits, by favor in contracts or financial operations, compel the manufacturer, the merchant, or the real producer, in order to preserve his rank in society, to seek for profits disproportionate to the services he renders to the production, then these other abuses tend to increase by other causes, the charges of production, and consequently the price of productions beyond their real utility.. The consumption of them is the more circumscribed; in order to obtain them we are obliged to give more productive services towards the creation of another production, and to go into larger expences of production. Judge, Sir, by this, of the evil that is done by encouraging useless expences and multiplying unproductive consumers.

What proves to how great an extent the costs of production are a real obstacle to the sale of productions, is the rapid sale of an article which an expeditious means of production puts at a low price. It is then obtained by every one with less labor and less charges of production of any sort. When in consequence of the continental system we were obliged to pay five francs for a pound of sugar, applied either to the production of the sugar itself or to any other commodity which was exchanged for the sugar. France could only purchase fourteen millions of pounds.[29] Now sugar is cheap we consume eighty millions of pounds yearly, which is nearly three pounds each person. At Cuba, where sugar is still cheaper, upwards of thirty pounds are consumed by each free person.[30]

Let is then admit a truth which stares us full in the face; that to levy excessive taxes, with or without the participation of a national representation, or with a derisive representation, it matters little, is increasing the charges of production, without increasing the utility of the production, and without adding anything to be satisfaction of a consumer in the use of them; is putting a fine upon production, *upon the existence of Society*. And as amongst producers some are better enabled than others, to throw upon their co-producers the burthen of circumstances, they affect some classes more than others. A capitalist oftentimes can withdraw his capital from one branch to employ it in another; or he may send it abroad. The enterpriser in a branch of industry has often fortune sufficient to suspend and the enterpriser are masters of their situations, the laborer is continually obliged to work at any price, even when the production no longer affords him wherewith to live. It is thus, Sir, that the excessive expences of production reduce many classes of certain nations, to consume no more than what is indispensably necessary to their existence, and the lower orders to perish for want. Now is not this, according to your own idea,[31] of all others the most desperate and barbarous means of reducing the number of mankind?[32]

Here, perhaps, the strongest objection presents itself, because it is supported by a striking example. In the United States hindrances to production are less numerous and the taxes light, and there, as elsewhere, commodities abound but commerce wants vent. - "The difficulties," you say[33] "cannot be attributed to the culture of bad land, nor to the hindrance so industry, nor the enormity of the taxes, wherefore, for the increase of wealth something more is necessary than the power of production." Alas! Would you believe it, Sir? In my opinion it is that very power of production, at least at the present, which is wanting to the United States, to enable the Americans advantageously to dispose of the superabundant productions of their commerce.

The happy situation of this people during a long war, in which they almost always enjoyed the advantages of neutrality, has given too forcible a direction of their activity and capitals towards maritime and foreign commerce. The Americans are enterprising, they carry cheap. They have introduced expeditious modes of navigation into their long voyages, which shortens them, renders them less expensive, and corresponds with those improvements which in the arts diminish the costs of production. In fact the Americans have drawn to their country all the maritime trade which the English could not do. They have for many years served as intermediate persons between all the continental powers of Europe and the rest of the world. They have even obtained greater success than the English, wherever they have been put in competition with them; for instance at China.

What is the consequence? An excessive abundance of those productions, which maritime and commercial industry procure; and when the general peace came, and restored the freedom of the seas, French and Dutch vessels precipitated themselves with a sort of delirium, into the midst of a route which had just been opened, and in their ignorance of the situation of foreign nations, of their agriculture, arts, population, and means of purchase and consumption, these vessels, escaped from a long detention, carried to all parts, in great abundance, the productions of the continent of Europe, presuming that the other countries of the world, which had been so long separated from it, would be most eager for them.

But in order to purchase this extraordinary supply, it would at the stone time have been necessary, that these countries on their part should have been able to have instantly created extraordinary productions: for again, the difficulty is not how to consume European commodities at New York, Baltimore, the Havannah, Rio Janeiro, or Buenos Ayres. They would very willingly consume them there, if they had' therewith to pay for them. Europeans require cotton, tobacco, sugar, and rice, in payment; and this demand enhances the price of them; and dear as these commodities and silver, which is also a commodity, were, you must either take them, or come away without payment; these same commodities become scarcer at the place of their origin, became more abundant in Europe, and finished by being too much so to sell well there; although the consumption in Europe is so much increased since the peace: hence the disadvantageous returns we have been witness to. But suppose for a moment that the agricultural and manufactured productions of North and South America were all at once become very considerable, when the peace took place; then their populations being more numerous and more productive, would easily have bought all that the Europeans carried there, and have given them sundry articles in return at a reasonable rate.

As to the United States, this will I have no doubt take place when they can add to the articles of Exchange with which their maritime commerce furnishes us[34] a greater quantity of agricultural produce, and perhaps also some manufactured articles. Their culture-is extending their manufactures, multiplying, and by a natural consequence their population increases with an astonishing rapidity. A few years more and their industry altogether will form a mass of productions, amongst which will be found articles fit to make profitable returns or at least profits, which the Americans will employ in the purchase of European commodities.

Those commodities which the Europeans succeed in making at least expence will be carried to America, and those which the American soil and industry succeed in creating at a lower rate than others, will be brought back. The nature of the demand will determine the nature of the productions; each nation will employ itself in preference about those productions in which they have the greatest success; that is, which they produce at least expence, and exchanges mutually and permanently advantageous will be the result. But these commercial improvements can only take place in the course of time. The talents and experience which the arts require are not acquired in a few months, years must be devoted to them. It will not be until after many experiments that the Americans will know what commodities they tan produce with success. Then those productions will no longer be tarried to their country; but the profit they will obtain from them will procure them the means of buying other European productions.

On the other hand, their agricultural enterprises, however rapid their extension may be, tan only by very slow degrees offer, by their productions, an opening to European productions. As cultivation and civilisation extend themselves beyond the Allegany Mountains in Kentucky, and into the Indiana and Illinois territories, the first gains are employed in feeding the colonies as they arrive from the states first peopled, and in building their habitations. The profits beyond these wants, serve to extend the clearing the woods, the next in manufacturing articles for local consumption; and it is only the savings of the fourth class which are applied in manufacturing the productions of the earth, and in transforming them for distant consumption. It is then only that new States present an opening to us Europeans; but it is evident this cannot be in their infancy: for that purpose it is necessary that their population should have had time to increase, and that their agricultural productions should have become so abundant, that they are under the necessity of seeking to exchange their value at a distance. Then, and by the natural progress of things, instead of transporting rough articles, they will transport articles which will have already received some shape, and which consequently containing a greater value in less compass, can bear the expences of a long voyage. Such productions will find their way to Europe through New Orleans, a city destined to be one of the greatest depots in the whole world.

We have not yet reached this point; is it then wonderful that the productions of the United States have not vet offered facilities analogous to the commercial ardor which followed the Peace? Is it even wonderful that commercial productions, brought by the Americans themselves into their ports, at the end of an exaggerated development of their nautical industry, should be found there in superabundance?

You see, Sir, that this fact has nothing in it that is not very conformable to the doctrine professed by your antagonists.

Reverting to the painful situation in which every kind of industry in Europe is at present, I might add to the discouragement which results from the costs of production multiplied to excess, the disorders which these costs occasion in the production, distribution, and consumption of value produced; disorders which frequently bring into the market quantities greater than the want, keeping back those that would sell, and whose owners would employ their price in the purchase of the former.

Certain producers seek to indemnify themselves by the quantity they produce, for a part of the value eat up by the taxes. Certain productive services find means to evade the avidity of the tax-gatherers, as often happens, for the service of capitals which in many instances continue to receive the same interest, whilst lands, houses, and industry, are surcharged. A workman who can with difficulty support his family, repurchases sometimes by excessive labor the low price of work. Are not these the causes which derange the natural course of production, and which occasion a production in some articles, beyond what would have been produced, had the wants of the consumers only been consulted? The articles of consumption are not necessary to us in equal degree. Previously to reducing our consumption of wheat to one half, we reduce that of meat to one quarter, and that of sugar to nothing. There are capitals so employed in certain enterprises, particularly in manufactures, that the enterprisers are frequently content to lose their interest and sacrifice the profits of their own industry, and continue to work solely for the purpose of keeping the enterprise going until more favorable times, and to preserve their funds; or they are afraid of losing good workmen, which the suspension of work would disperse: and humanity alone is sufficient to induce enterprisers to continue a manufactory for whose productions there is no longer any demand. From whence proceed disorders in the progress of production and consumption, still greater than those which proceed from the obstruction of the customs and the vicissitudes of the Seasons. Hence proceed unadvised productions, recourse to ruinous means, and a ruined commerce.

I shall remark at the same time, that although the evil is great it may still seem greater than it is. The commodities which superabound in the markets of the universe, may strike the eye by their mass, and alarm commerce by the depredation of their price, and still be only a very small part of the commodities made and consumed of each kind. There is no warehouse that would not be very soon emptied, if every kind of production of the commodity contained in it was simultaneously to cease in all parts of the world.

It has been further remarked, that if the quantity sent in the slightest degree exceeds the want, it is sufficient to alter the price considerably. It was a remark of *Addison*, in his Spectator, (No. 200,) that when the wheat harvest exceeds by one-tenth the ordinary consumption, wheat falls one half in price. Dalrymple[35] makes an analogous observation. We must therefore not be astonished, that a slight excess is often taken for an excessive abundance.

This superabundance, as I have already remarked, depends also upon the ignorance of producers or merchants, of the nature and extent of the want in the places to which they sent their commodities. In later years there have been a number of hazardous speculations, on account of the many fresh connexions with different nations. There was every where a general failure of that calculation which was requisite to a good result; but because many things have been ill done does it follow that it is impossible, with better instruction, to do better? I dare predict, that as the new connexions grow old, and as reciprocal wants are better appreciated, the excess of commodities will everywhere cease; and that a mutual and profitable intercourse will be established. But in the mean time it will. be proper gradually, and as much as the circumstances of each State will permit, to diminish the general and permanent inconveniences which arise from too expensive a production. We must fully convince ourselves that everyone will sell his productions more easily, in proportion as others gain; that there is only one way of getting, which is either by our labor or by the labor of the capital and land we possess; that unproductive consumers are only substitutes for productive consumers; that 'the more producers there are the more consumers there are; that for the same reason, each nation is interested in the prosperity of the rest, and that they are altogether interested in having easy communications; for every difficulty is equivalent to an increase of expence.

Such is the doctrine established in my works, and which I confess to you, Sir, does not hitherto appear to me to have been shaken. I have taken up the pen in defence of it, not because it is mine, (What is the sorry self-love of an author in comparison with things of so great importance?) but because it is to a high degree social, that it shows to mankind the source of real wealth, and warns them of the danger of corrupting that source.

The rest of this doctrine is not less useful, in as much as it shows us that capital and land are not productive, unless they become property sacred to the proprietors. That even the poor themselves are interested in defending the property of the rich, and consequently in the maintenance of good order; because a subversion, which never could do more than give them a fleeting prey, would take away from him a constant income. When Political Economy is studied as it ought to be; when we once begin to perceive in the course of this study, that the most wholesome truths rest upon the most certain principles, we have nothing so much at heart as to place these principles within the reach of every comprehension. Do not let us increase their natural difficulties by useless abstractions; do not let us repeat the ridiculous performances of the economists of the 18th century, by endless discussions on the net produce of the earth. Let us describe the mode in which things take place, and explain the chain which connects them. Then our writings will acquire a great practical utility, and the public will be really indebted to those writers who, like yourself, Sir, have so great means of giving them information.

LETTER THE FOURTH.

SIR,

I have sought in your *Principles of Political Economy*, for something wherewith to confirm the opinion of the public, relative to machines, and generally relatively to expeditious processes, which, in the arts, shorten manual labor and multiply productions without increasing the expence of production. I should wish to find in them those fixed principles, that rigorous mode of reasoning which carries conviction with it, and to which your *Essay on Population* has accustomed the public. But this is not an Essay on Population. It appears to me, (for I am sometimes reduced to the necessity of making use of this form, after having read your demonstrations) it appears to me that all the advantage you admit in machinery, and generally in expeditious means of production, is reduced to the fact of multiplying productions to such an extent, that even when their selling value is lessened the total amount still exceeds what it was before the improvement.[36] The advantage you point out is incontrovertible; and it has been already remarked, that the total value of cotton goods, as well as the total number of workmen employed in this branch, had singularly increased since the introduction of expeditious means. An analogous remark had been made relative to the printing press; this machine employed in the multiplication of books, a production which employs at this moment, without reckoning the authors, a much greater number of persons than when they were copied by hand, and which is worth a much larger sum than when books were dearer.

But this very decided advantage, is only one among the many which nations have reaped by the employment of machinery. It only relates to certain productions, the consumption of which was susceptible of sufficient extension to balance the diminution in their price, whilst there is an advantage in the introduction of machines common to all economical and expeditious processes in general; an advantage which would be felt even when the consumption of the production should be no longer capable of any extension; an advantage which ought to be highly valued in the *principles* of Political Economy. Have the goodness to excuse me, if, in order to make myself understood, I am obliged to revert to a few elementary ideas.

Machines and *tools* are both productions, which immediately after their production rank in the class of capital, and are employed in the perfection of other productions. The only difference there is between machines and tools, is that the former are complex tools, and the latter simple machines. As there are no machines or tools existing which engender force we must still consider them as the means of transmitting an action, an active force of which we dispose, towards an object which is to be modified by it. Thus a hammer is a tool by means whereof we employ the muscular strength of a man in flattening, in certain cases a leaf of gold; and the mill hammers of a large forge are also tools by means whereof we employ a fall of water in flattening iron bars.

The employ of a voluntary force, with which Nature has gifted us, does not deprive it of its nature of a tool. The weight increased by velocity, which constitutes the power of a gold beater's hammer, is not less a natural physical power than the weight of the water which falls from a mountain.

What is our industry altogether, but the employ, more or less understood, of the laws of Nature. It is *by obeying Nature*, says Bacon, that *we learn to command it.* What difference do you see between knitting needles and a stocking frame, except that the latter is a more complicated and a more powerful tool than the needles; but for the rest, employing with greater or less advantage the properties of the metal, and the power of the lever to manufacture the articles with which we cover our legs and feet.

The question then resolves itself to this: it is an advantage to man to take in his hand a more powerful tool, capable of doing much more work, or of doing it better, rather than a still larger but imperfect tool, with which he works slower with more difficulty and not so well.

I think I should offer an insult to your good sense and to that of our readers, if I doubted the answer a moment.

The perfection of our tools, Sir, is connected with the perfection of our species. It is that which makes the difference which is observable between us and the savages of the South Seas, who have axes of flint, and sewing needles made of fish bones.

It is no longer admissible, for anyone who writes upon Political Economy to endeavor to circumscribe the introduction of the means which chance or genius may put into our hands, with a view of preserving more work for our laborers; such a one would expose himself to have all his own arguments made use of to prove to him that we ought, (retrograding instead of advancing in the career of civilisation) successively to renounce all the discoveries we have already made, and to render our arts more imperfect in order to multiply our labor by diminishing our enjoyments.

No doubt there are inconveniences in the transit from one order of things to another, even from an imperfect to a better order. What person in his senses would all at once take off the shackles which obstruct industry, and remove the Custom Houses which separate nations, prejudicial as they are to their prosperity? In these eases the duty of well informed persons does not consist in producing motives for keeping back and proscribing every kind of change, under pretence of the inconveniences they carry with them; but in appreciating these inconveniences, in pointing out the practicable means of preventing or diminishing them as much as possible, for the purpose of facilitating the adoption of a desirable amendment.

The inconveniences in this ease is a removal of income, which when it is sudden, is more or less injurious to the class whose income it diminishes. The substitution of machinery diminishes (sometimes, but not always,) the income of the class whose funds consist of corporeal and manual faculties, to augment the income of the class whose funds consist in intellectual faculties and in capitals. In other words, expeditious machines, being in general more complex, require more considerable capitals; consequently they compel the enterpriser who employs them to purchase more of what we have called productive service of capital, and less of what we call productive services of laborers. At the same time, as perhaps they require greater attention and more care in their general and particular management, they employ more of that kind of productive service from whence the enterpriser's income proceeds. A cotton spinner who uses the small wheel, as we see in many places in Normandy, scarcely deserves the name of enterpriser, whilst a large wholesale cotton manufactory is an enterprise of magnitude.

But the most important effect, although perhaps the least perceptible, which proceeds from the employment of machinery in general, of all other expeditious processes, is the increase of income which results from them to the consumers of their productions; an increase which costs nothing to anybody, and of which it is worthwhile to give some detail.

If wheat were pounded in our days, as it was by the ancients, by the strength of the arm, I apprehend it would take twenty men to grind as much flour as one pair of stones in a mill can grind. These twenty men, in the neighbourhood of Paris, being continually employed, would cost 40 francs per day, at 300 days' work in the year they would cost per year fr.. 12,000

The machine and the stones cost suppose 20,000 fr. a year's interest on which would be - - - 1,000

No enterpriser would probably be found to undertake such an enterprise, unless it brought him in yearly about - 3,000

The cost, therefore, of the flour that may be obtained from a pair of stones in one year would, by this means, amount to about .... fr. 10,000

Instead of which a miller now a days can hire a windmill for - 2,000

He pays his man - - 1,000

I suppose he gains for his labor and abilities - - - 3,000

The same quantity of flour can therefore be ground for - - - fr. 6;000 instead of 16,000, which it would have cost if we still followed the custom of our ancestors.

The same population can be fed, for the mill does not diminish the quantity of flour ground: the profit gained in society serves to pay for fresh productions, for the moment the 6,000 francs cost of production are paid, a profit of 6,000 francs is gained; and society enjoys this essential advantage, that mankind who compose it, whatever be their means of existence or their income, whether they live upon their labor, their capital, or their stock of land, reduce the portion of their expences destined to the payment of the cost of the flour in the proportion of sixteen to six or five-eighths. He who spent eight francs annually for his food would only spend three, which is exactly equal to an increase of income; for the five francs saved in this article can be employed in any other. If an equal improvement had taken place in all the productions in which we employ our incomes, they would really have been increased five eighth; and a man who gains three thousand francs, either in making flour, or in any other manner, would actually be as rich as if he had eight thousand and the improved method had not been discovered.

M. Sismondi has not .aid attention to this, when he wrote the following passage.

"Every time," he says,[37] "that the demand for consumption exceeds the means of the population to produce, every new discovery in mechanism or the arts is a benefit to society, because it gives the means of satisfying existing wants. Every time, on the contrary, that the production is fully adequate to the consumption every such discovery is a calamity, because it only adds to the enjoyment of consumers by satisfying them at a cheaper rate, whilst it suppresses the life itself of the producers. It would be odious to weigh the advantage of a cheap rate against that of existence."

M. Sismondi, as appears, does not sufficiently appreciate the advantage of a cheap rate, and does not feel that by giving less for one article we can afford to give more for another, beginning with the most indispensable.

Up to this time no inconvenience is perceptible in the invention of flour mills, but the advantage of a diminution in the price of the production is very visible, which is equal to an increase of income to all those who use them.

But this increase of income procured for the consumers, is taken away from the nineteen unfortunate men whom the mill has thrown out of work. This I deny. The nineteen laborers have their industrious faculties left, with the same strength, the same capacities, the same means of labor as before. The mill does not compel them to remain unemployed, but only to seek another occupation. Many circumstances occasion a similar inconvenience without carrying with them the same remedy.

A fashion out of use, a war which blocks up a vent, a commerce which changes its course, do a hundred times more injury to the laboring classes than any new invention whatever.

I suppose that it will be said and insisted on, that the nineteen vacant laborers, supposing even they immediately find capitals to set them to work at a fresh business, could not sell their production because the mass of production of society would be thereby increased, but not the amount of their income. It has then been forgotten that the incomes of society are increased by the very fact of the production of the nineteen new laborers. The salary for their labor is the income which enables them to acquire the produce of their labor, or to exchange it against any other equivalent production: this is sufficiently established in my preceding letters.

Nothing therefore remains, strictly speaking, but the inconvenience of being obliged to change the occupation. Now the progress which is made in one kind in particular, is beneficial to industry in general. The increase of income, which results to society from a saving in expences, is carried towards other articles. A single occupation is interdicted to nineteen men who, till then, pounded grain, and a hundred fresh occupations, or a hundred extensions of old occupations, have been opened to them. I desire no other proof of this than the increase which has taken place in the labor and population, in every place where the arts have been improved. The constant habit we are in of seeing the productions of new arts causes us to disregard them, but how would they strike our ancestors, if they could again come amongst us! Let us picture to ourselves for a moment some of the most enlightened amongst them, such as Pliny or Archimedes, coming to walk round one of our modern cities; they would fancy themselves surrounded by miracles. The abundance of our crystals and glasses, the great quantity of our large mirrors, our docks, watches, embroidery, iron bridges, warlike instruments, and ships, would astonish them beyond all conception. And if they were to go into our work-shops, what a multiplicity of occupations would they see of which they could not have the smallest conception. Would they even believe that thirty thousand men were nightly employed in Europe in printing newspapers, which are read every morning over the breakfast-table whilst taking tea, coffee, chocolate, or other food, quite as new to them as the papers themselves? Do not let us doubt, Sir, that if the arts still improve, as I flatter myself they will, that is, that they will produce more at less expence, fresh millions of men in the course of a few ages will produce objects, which would excite in our minds, could we see them, a surprise equal to that which the great Archimedes and Pliny would experience could they revisit us. Let us take care, we who scribble in search of truth, if our writings descend to posterity, that the apprehension with which those improvements inspire us (but which they will then have far surpassed) do not appear ridiculous. And as to the workmen of your country, at once so able and so wretched, our descendants may well look upon them as men who were compelled to get their living by dancing on the rope, with a weight attached to their feet. They will read in history, that in order that these men might continue their dance, some fresh plan was daily suggested to them, indeed every plan except the very one which would have been efficacious, viz. that of taking off the weight: then our descendants after having derided us might very well conclude the whole by pitying us.

I have said that a useful improvement may be attended with temporary inconvenience; fortunately those inconveniences which are occasioned by expeditious processes, are mitigated by some circumstances which have been already noticed, and by others of which no mention has been made. It has been said (and you yourself, Sir, look upon this circumstance as capable of over balancing the inconvenience) that the low price which results from an economical process favors the consumption of the article to so great a degree, that the same production employs more people than before; as has been remarked in spinning and weaving cotton. I shall add that, as machinery and expeditious means increase, it will be more difficult to discover fresh ones, particularly in an established art in which workmen are already initiated. The most simple machines appeared first, afterwards came the more complicated: they cost more to erect, and require more workmen to manoeuvre them, which partly recompenses that class for the occupation they have lost in the adoption of the new process. The complexity and costliness of a machine are obstacles to its too prompt adoption. The cloth shearing machine by means of a turning motion, cost in the origin from 25 to 30 thousand francs. Many manufacturers cannot in the first instance lay out such a sum, others consider and reconsider before they buy it, and await for a decided proof of its success. This tardiness in the introduction of new machines nearly prevents all the inconveniences attending them.

In fact, I confess to you, that in practice I have always seen new machines occasion more fear of harm, than harm itself. As to the good, it is sure and lasting.

M. de Sismondi opposes a fact that occurred, in which a hundred thousand stocking-knitters with their needles, and a thousand workmen provided with frames, each manufactured ten thousand pair of stockings. The result was, that in the latter case the consumers of stockings only saved 50 centimes per pair, and still a manufactory which used to employ a hundred thousand work-people, now only employed twelve hundred. But he only comes to this conclusion by suppositions which are not admissible.

To prove that consumers obtained the stockings only 50 centimes less, he supposes that the cost of production would be, in the first case, as follows:

10 millions, for the purchase of the material.

40 millions, wages to a hundred thousand work-people, at 400 francs each.

Total 50 millions, 40 of which paid to the work-people.

And in the second ease, he supposes the cost as follows:

10 millions, for the material.

30 millions, for interest of fixed capital and enterpriser's profits.

2 millions, for interest of circulating capital.

2 millions, for repairs and new machines.

1 million, wages of 1200 workmen.

Total 45 millions, of which 1 is paid to the workmen instead of 40.

Now I see that this item of 30 millions for interest of fixed capital, and enterpriser's profit, taken on the supposition of an enterprise capable of employing twelve hundred work-people, and of yielding 15 per cent on their capitals, supposes a capital of two hundred millions, a supposition truly preposterous.

One workman cannot work at two frames at once, a thousand workmen would therefore require a thousand frames to be employed. A good stocking-frame costs 600 francs, consequently the thousand would cost six hundred thousand francs; add to this capital, a like capital for the other utensils, work-shops, etc. still we should only have occasion for a capital of twelve hundred thousand francs. We admit that the interest and the enterpriser's profit on the capital would be 15 per cent, which is very moderate, for a current business which produced more would soon by competition be brought to this rate. Admitting this, we shall find for the interest and the enterpriser's profit, 180 thousand francs, instead of 30 millions!

The same observation applies to the 2 millions for expences of keeping and repairing the machines; for if, instead of repairing the frames, new ones were bought yearly, still they would only cost 600 thousand francs.

Nor would the circulating capital cost 2 millions, for in Mr. Sismondi's hypothesis, of what does it consist? Of the raw material, which he quotes at 10 millions, and wages, which he calls 1 million, together 11 millions, the interest of which, at 5 per cent, is 550 thousand francs. But as in this business the production may be completed and sold within 6 months, the capital paid for if the author has quoted the capital for the machines cost each time 275 thousand francs, instead of 2 millions.

All these expences together still only make 12,055,000 francs, instead of 50 millions, which stockings knit with the needle would cost, according to M. Sismondi. I am far from thinking that the saving could be so great, for if the author has quoted the capital for the machines too high, he has attributed too great a facility to them, in supposing that by their means twelve hundred workmen could do as much as a hundred thousand; but I say that if the saving in this production were so great, the low price of stockings or any other article of that nature would so favor the consumption, that instead of seeing the hundred thousand work-people, as is supposed, employed, we should probably see the number increase to two hundred thousand.

And if the consumption of this article in particular, .did not admit this excessive multiplication of the same production, the demand would increase in respect to many others; for observe, that after the introduction of machinery, the same revenue is still found in society, that is, the same number of workmen, the same amount .of capital, and the same portion of land. Now if, instead of devoting out of this mass of revenue 50 millions yearly for stockings, it is only necessary, in consequence of the frames, to employ 12, the 38 millions remaining may be applied to other consumptions, if not to the extension of this.

This is what principles teach, and experience confirms. The misery suffered by the population of England, and which M. Sismondi deplores with a truly philanthropic feeling, arises from other causes, principally from the poor laws, and, as I have hinted, from a weight of taxation which makes production too expensive; so much so, that when the articles are finished, a great part of the consumers do not get sufficient to obtain them, at the price that is obliged to be asked for them.

LETTER THE FIFTH.

SIR,

On reading your *Principles of Political Economy*, the first object which struck my attention was that great evil which torments the human race, and prevents them from living on their productions. Although in the order of ideas, a discussion on the nature of wealth ought to precede this, in order to assist the mind in comprehending all the phenomena which relate to its formation and distribution, I have not thought it right to give it the preference, as it appears to be more peculiarly interesting to those who cultivate the science of political economy, without any view of carrying it into practice. Still I cannot lay down my pen without giving you my opinion on this head. I have your own sanction for so doing, in the noble candor with which you invite every discussion that may tend to enlighten the public. "It is to be desired," you say, (page 4) "that those who are looked upon by the public to be competent judges should agree upon the principal points." They cannot be made too clear.

You complain of the definition which Lord Lauderdale gives of wealth, when he says that "it is everything man can desire, that can be useful or agreeable to him," as being too vague, and I think you are very right. I am seeking the definition which you think ought to be substituted for this, and I find that you give the term wealth to "all material objects that are necessary, useful, or agreeable to man" (page 28). The only difference I see between these two definitions consists in the word material, which you add to that of my Lord Lauderdale, and I must confess that this word appears to me to be contrary to the truth.

You will anticipate my reasons. The great discovery of political economy, and what will render it everlastingly precious, is the having shown that everything may be converted into wealth. From that time man has been made capable of knowing what it is necessary for him to do, to attain these happy means of satisfying his desires. But as I have formerly had occasion to observe, it is beyond the power of man to add a single atom to the mass of matter, of which the world is composed. If he creates wealth, wealth is not matter: there is no medium. By means of his capital and his land, man can only change the combination of matter, to confer utility upon it, but utility is an immaterial quality.

This is not all, Sir; I fear your definition does not contain the essential character of wealth. Allow me to give a few explanations in support of my idea.

Adam Smith and all the world have observed, that a glass of water, which is a very precious thing when we are thirsty, was not wealth. It is however a material object, it is either necessary, useful, or agreeable to man. It fulfils all the conditions of your definition, and it is not wealth. At least not that wealth which is the subject of our study, and that of your book. What is wanting to make it so possessing value?

There are things indeed which are natural wealth, very precious to man, but which are not of that kind .about which political economy can be employed. Can it increase them? Can it consume them? No, they are subject to other laws. A glass of water is under the government of natural law. The attachment of our friends, and our reputation in the world, depend upon the moral law, and not on that of political economy. What then is wealth, the main spring of this science? that which is susceptible of creation and destruction, of more and of less; and this more, this less, what is it against value.

You yourself, Sir, are obliged to confess it in many places. You say (page 340,) "It appears therefore, that the wealth of a nation depends partly on the quantity of production obtained by its labor, (it depends on this altogether,) and partly on the adaptation of this labor to the wants and means of the population, for the purpose of giving value to its productions." And in the following page, you are still more positive. After having gone further into the question, you admit that, "it is evident that in the present state of things, the value of commodities may be considered as the only cause of the existence of wealth." How can it be then, that so essential an ingredient as value, is wanting to your definition?

But that is not sufficient: we should know but very imperfectly the nature of wealth, if we were not well to define this word value. In order to possess great wealth, is it enough that we value our possessions very high? If I have, built a house which I find delightful, and think it might to estimate it at a hundred thousand francs, am I really worth a hundred thousand francs on account of this house? We receive a present from a person who is dear to us, which is inestimable in our eyes - does it follow that that makes us immensely rich? You cannot think so. In order for a value to be riches, it must be an admitted value; not by the possessor, but by another person. Now what irresistible proof can be given, that a value is admitted, if not, that in order to have it, other persons consent to give in exchange a certain quantity of other things, which are valuable.

Notwithstanding I may have estimated my house at a hundred thousand francs, what shall I have made of it, if I can find no one who will give me more than fifty thousand of those pieces which we call francs. It is in fact worth no more than fifty thousand, it makes me worth no more than fifty thousand, or whatever may be bought for fifty thousand francs.

Thus Adam Smith,[38] immediately after having observed that there are two sorts of values, one value in use, the other value in exchange, completely abandons the first, and entirely occupies himself all the way through his book with exchangeable value only. This is what you yourself have done, Sir;[39] what Mr. Ricardo has done; what I have done; what we have all done: for this reason, that there is no other value in political economy than that which alone is subject to fixed laws; that that alone forms, distributes, and destroys itself conformably to invariable rules, which may become the subject of a scientific study. By a necessary consequence, the price of each article being its exchangeable value in money, there are no other than current prices in political economy. What Smith calls natural prices have nothing more natural in them, than all the rest. It is the cost of production, the price current of productive services.

I do not pretend to deny that you have in Mr. Ricardo a powerful and respectable auxiliary. He was against you in the question of Vent, he contends with you on the question of Value, but notwithstanding my connexion with him, and the mutual esteem we entertain for each other, I have not hesitated to combat his opinions.[40] Our first inclination for each other, and I am bold to say yours and mine also, was it not for the sake of the public good and of truth?

These are Mr. Ricardo's words: "Value is essentially different from wealth, for value does not depend upon the abundance (of the things necessary or it agreeable) but on the difficulty or facility of their production. The manufactural labor of a million of persons will always produce the stone value, but not always the same wealth. By more perfect machines, a more practised ability, a better divided labor, the opening of fresh markets giving rise to more advantageous exchanges, a million persons may produce double and treble the quantity of necessary or agreeable things, than they could produce in another social situation, and still they would add nothing to the total value."[41]

This argument, founded on uncontested facts, appears perfectly to agree with the opinion you maintain. The question is, how these facts strengthen instead of weaken the doctrine of value, the doctrine which establishes, that wealth consists in the value of the things we possess; confining this word value to the only admitted and exchangeable value.

In fact what is value, but that quality susceptible of appreciation, susceptible of more or less, which is inherent in the things we possess. It is the quality which enables us to obtain the things we want, in exchange for the things we have. This value is the greater, in proportion to the quantity which the thing we have can obtain of that we want; for instance, when I have occasion to change my horse for wheat, if my horse is worth six hundred francs, I shall receive double the quantity of bushels of wheat than if he were worth only three hundred francs, and at the same time that part of my wealth would be double. And as the same reasoning may he generally applied to all I possess, it follows that our wealth depends on the value of the things we possess. This is a consequence that no one can reasonably refuse to admit.

You cannot on your part deny, says Mr. Ricardo to me, that we are not richer, when we have more of the necessary or agreeable things to consume, whatever may be their value in another sense. This in fact I admit, but is it not to have more things to consume, having the power to acquire them in greater quantity? To possess more wealth is to have in our hands wherewith to buy a larger quantity of useful things, a greater quantity of utility, in extending this expression to everything that is necessary or agreeable to us. Now there is nothing in this proposition, which is contrary to what is true in the definition which Mr. Ricardo and yourself give of wealth. You say that *wealth* is in the quantity of necessary or agreeable things we possess. I say so too, but as these words, *quantity of necessary or agreeable things*, have a vague and arbitrary meaning, which cannot be admitted in a good definition, I define them by their exchangeable value; then the limitation of the idea of utility is the being equal to any other utility, which other persons consent to give in exchange for that you possess; from that time there is equation, one value can be compared with another by the means of a third. A sack of wheat is a riches equal to a piece of cloth, when one can be exchanged against the other for an equal number of crowns. This will serve as a basis for comparisons, will admit of measuring an augmentation, or a diminution -- in a word, this is the basis of a science. Without this, political economy does not exist. It is this consideration alone which has brought it to light: it is so essential, that you involuntarily do it homage, and there is no one of your arguments in which it is not either expressed or understood; otherwise, you would have caused the science to recede, instead of enriching it with fresh truths.

At the same time that your and Mr. Ricardo's definition fails in precision, it fails also in extent. It does not embrace the whole of what our wealth is composed of. What! Our wealth confined to material objects either necessary or agreeable! And our talents? What then do you take these for? Are they not productive funds? Do we not derive income from them? Greater or less incomes, the same as we derive a greater income from an acre of good land than from an acre of brambles? I know some clever artists, who have no other income than what they derive from their talents, and who are opulent: according to your idea they would be no richer than a mere dauber.

You cannot deny it, that everything that has an exchangeable value makes part of our riches. They are essentially composed of the productive funds we possess. These funds are either land, capital, or personal faculties. Of these funds some are alienable, as land; others are alienable and consumable, as capital; others inalienable, and yet consumable, as talents, which perish with their possessor. From these funds proceed all the revenues which keep society alive, and what appears paradoxical, although perfectly true, all these revenues are immaterial, since they are derived from an immaterial quality which is utility. The different utilities produced by our productive funds are compared with each other by their value, which I have no occasion to call *exchangeable*, because in political economy I recognize no other than exchangeable.

As to the difficulty Mr. Ricardo makes, when he says that, by better understood processes, a thousand persons may produce twice and three times as much wealth without producing more value, this is no difficulty, when we consider, (as we ought) production as an exchange, in which the productive services of our labor, our land, and capital are given in order to obtain productions. By means of these productive services, we acquire all the productions that are in the world, and this by the bye is what gives value to productions; for, after having obtained them by giving value for them, we cannot give them away for nothing. Now since our first property is the productive funds we possess, our first revenue the productive services which proceed from them, we are richer in proportion as our productive services are more valuable, as they obtain in the exchange called production, a greater or less quantity of useful things. And at the same time, as a greater quantity of useful things and their low price, are perfectly synonymous expressions, the producers are rich, when productions are more abundant and cheaper. I say producers in general, because competition compels them to give their productions for what they cost them; so that when producers of wheat or cloth succeed by help of the same productive services in producing a double quantity of wheat or cloth, all the other producers can purchase a double quantity of wheat or cloth with a like quantity of productive services, or what is the same thing, with the produce they derive from them.

Such, Sir, is the well-connected doctrine, without which I declare it to be impossible to explain the greatest difficulties of political economy, and particularly how a nation can be richer, when its productions diminish in value, although riches are value. You see that I am not afraid to reduce my pretended paradoxes to their simple expression. I strip them naked, and trust them to your equity, to that of Mr. Ricardo, and to the good sense of the public. But at the same time reserving to myself the right of explaining them, if they are ill understood, and of defending them boldly if unjustly attacked.

NOTES

1. The Translation of Professor Malthus's *Principles of Political Economy*, by M. F. S. Constancie, (who translated Mr. Ricardo's work) is in the press, and will appear in the course of the month of August, published by J. P. Aillaud, Bookseller, No. 21, Quai Voltaire. It will consist of two octavo volumes, of about 400 pages each.

2. Sismondi's *New Principles of Political Economy*, vol. i. 337, and following pages.

3. Malthus's Principles of Political Economy, page 354. (I quote from the English Edition, not having yet seen a translation).

4. *Treatise on Political Economy*, or simple explanation of the manner in which riches are obtained, distributed and consumed, 4th edition. Vol. ii. page 5.

5. Malthus's *Principles* etc. page 353.

6. What oftentimes makes English authors obscure is, that they confound by the example of Smith, under the name of labor, the services rendered by men, by capital, and by land.

7. A domestic produces personal services, which, as soon as produced, are unproductively consumed by his master. The service of a public functionary is also entirely consumed by the public, as it is produced. This is the reason why these different services do not produce any augmentation of wealth. The consumer enjoys these services but cannot accumulate them. This is particularly explained in my *Treatise on Political Economy*, 4th Ed. vol. i. page 124. How Mr. Malthus could print page 35 after

this, is inconceivable: in which he says that, "the progress which Europe has made since the feudal times cannot be explained, if per anal service is considered as productive as the labor of tradesmen and manufacturers. It is the same with these services as with the labor of the gardener who has cultivated salads or strawberries. The wealth of Europe certainly does not proceed from the strawberries, because they, like personal service, are all unproductively consumed as they ripen, although not so quick as personal service.

I mention strawberries here, as a produce of very short duration, but it is not because a production is durable that it gives greater facility to accumulation. It is because it is so consumed as to produce its value in another article: for durable or not. every production is devoted to consumption, and is no further useful than by its consumption (this utility consists, either in satisfying a want, or in producing a fresh value). When we begin to write upon political economy, the first thing to be done is to divest ourselves of the idea that a durable production accumulates better than a perishable one.

8. What the English call Want and Supply.

9. Fourth edition. Bk. I. ch. 15. Bk. II ch. l. 2. 3 and 5. See also the Epitome at tho end of each work, particularly the words *Productive Services, Charges of Production, Revenues, Profit, Value.*

10. Malthus's *Principles of Political Economy*, page 351.

11. A farmer who sells a sack of wheat for 30 francs, and buys a piece of calico for 30 francs, does he not exchange his wheat for the cloth? and the manufacturer who buys a

sack of wheat for 30 francs, the price of his piece of cloth, does he not exchange his cloth for a sack of wheat?

12. That I may not be accused of having perverted the estimable Professor's meaning, by endeavouring to compress it and render it clearer, I have thought it right to annex an exact translation of his words in a note.

"If commodities were only to be compared and exchanged one with another, it would then be true that if they increased in convenient proportions, they might, whatever was their increase preserve the same relative value. But if we compare them as we ought, with the number and wants of consumers, a great increase of production with a stationary number of consumers, and

wants reduced by parsimony, would of necessity occasion a great fall in the value of the productions estimated in labor, so that the same production which costs the same labor as heretofore could no longer purchase the same quantity of it." Page 355.

"It is said that an effective demand is nothing more than the effective supply which is produced of one commodity in exchange for another. But is this all that is really necessary to an effective demand?

"Although each of the commodities may have cost in producing it, the same portion of labor and capital, and that the one is equivalent to the other, still they may both be so abundant as not to he capable of purchasing more labor than they cost, or at least but very little more than they cost. In this case would the demand be effective? Certainly not." ibid.

13. Agreeably to the English expression, When they do not command the same quantity of labor as before.

14. This demonstration by the bye completely ruins an *assertion of Mr. Malthus that a low price is always at the expence of profit*, (page 370) and consequently ruins all the reasoning rounded upon that basis. The same demonstration is equally fatal to all that part of Mr. Ricardo's doctrine in which he flatters himself to have established, that the cost of production, and not the proportion of the supply to the demand, regulates the price of productions. He identifies the cost of productions with the productions, whilst they are opposite, and the former are the less in proportion as the latter are more abundant.

15. Some persons imagine that, when a capital is employed in an enterprise, that portion of it which is devoted to the purchase of the first materials is not employed in the purchase of productive services. This is an error. The first materials themselves are a produce which have no other value which has previously been spread by the productive services which have made a produce and a value of them. When the first materials are of no value they employ no part of the capital. When they must be paid for, this payment is no other than the reimbursement of the productive services which have given them their value.

16. The profits which an enterpriser makes of his enterprise, are the salary of the labor and talents he has employed in it. He carries on this enterprise no longer than this salary is such that he could not hope for a better in another enterprise. He is one of the necessary producers, and his profits are part of the necessary expenses of production.

17. This case is much more frequent in France than in England, where the rate of the profits of industry and the interest of capital are too low in the ordinary occupations of industry for the former to maintain a family, that has no capital.

18. What an accumulation of productions. What a prodigious vent according to Mr. Say, says Mr. Malthus, would such an event open. The learned professor totally mistakes in this case the meaning of the word accumulation; an accumulation is not a non-consumption it is the substitution of a reproductive for an unproductive consumption. Besides I did not say that a produce saved was a vent opened. I said that a produce created was a vent opened for another produce, and that is true whether the value of it is spent unproductively, or added to the savings, that is, to the reproductive expences which are proposed to be made.

19. It must be admitted that produce saved yearly is as regularly consumed as that which is expended yearly, but that it is consumed by other persons. Mr. Malthus's *Principles of Economy*. page 31.

20. "When there are more capitals in a country than are wanted, to recommend saving, is contrary to every principle of Political Economy. It is like recommending marriages to a people dying of hunger." *Principles d Political Economy*, page 495.

21. The principal obstacles to agricultural improvements in France, are in the first place the residence of rich proprietors and large capitalists in the towns and particularly in an immense capital: they cannot take account of amendments in which they might employ their lands: and they cannot inspect the employment of them so

that it may be followed with a corresponding increase of income. In the second place, it would be in vain that any canton in the heart of the country should double its productions, for it ear scarcely get rid of what it already produces, for want of good roads in the neighbourhood and for want of industrious towns within reach. Industrious towns consume rural productions, and manufacture in exchange manufactural productions, which containing greater value in less compass, can be transmitted to a greater distance. This is the chief obstacle to the increase of French agriculture. Small and numerous navigation canals, roads in good condition, would increase the value of rural productions. But to accomplish this local administration chosen by the inhabitants, whose only care should be the good of the neighbourhood, would be necessary. The possibility of vent exists, but all that may be done to benefit by it is not done. Managers in the interest of the central authority almost all become political or financial' agents, or what is still worse police-agents.

22. *Travels in France*, vol. 2, page 98, Engl. Edition.

23. This supposition is very admissible, for in England three parts of the population live in towns. and consequently are not employed in country labors. A country therefore which feeds 60 million inhabitants. may be very well cultivate by 15 million cultivators. the number which is computed in France at the present day.

24. The means we have of attaining, are the profits which every one obtains from his industry, his capital. and land. Consumers, who have neither industry, nor capital, nor land, spend what they take away from the profit of the former. In every ease each person has an income which has a limit. and although those persons who have a very large income can sacrifice large sums of money for very trifling

pleasures, still it may be conceived the dearer the pleasure the less it is sought after.

25. If he diminishes the quality, it is the same as if he raised the price.

26. New Principles, book iv, chap. 4.

27. The workman can only continue to work so long as he can subsist by his labor; and when his subsistence is too dear, it is not convenient to any enterpriser to employ him. Then it may be said, in Political Economy. that the workman no longer .supplies his productive labor, although he offers it with great earnestness; but this offer is not acceptable on the only durable conditions on which it can be performed.

28. Mr. Ricardo pretends that in spite of taxes and other obstructions, there is always as much industry as capital employed and that all capitals saved are still employed because capitalists will not lose the interest. There are, on the contrary, many savings unemployed on account of the difficulty in employing them, or being employed are lost in consequence of bad management. Besides, Mr. Ricardo is contradicted by what happened to us in 1813, when the faults of the government ruined all commerce, and when interest of money fell so low, for want of good opportunities of employing it -- and by what is happening to us at this moment in which the capitals sleep at the bottom of the coffers of capitalists. -- The Bank of France alone has 223 millions in specie in its coffers; a sum. more than double the amount of the notes in circulation, and six times greater than prudence warrants to be kept for casual payments.

29. See the report upon the situation of France, made in 1813, by the then Minister of the Interior. He was interested in disguising this decline of commerce

30. Humbolt's Essay on New Spain, vol. iii, page 183.

31. See Malthus's Essay on Population, book ii, chap. 11, of the French translation, and chap. 13 of the 5th English edition.

32. Mr Malthus, still convinced that there are classes who render service to society simply by consuming without producing, would consider it a misfortune if the whole or a great part of the English national debt were paid off. This circumstance would, on the contrary, in my opinion be very favorable for England, because the result would be that the stock-holder, being paid off, would obtain some income from their capitals. That those who pay taxes would themselves spend the 40 millions sterling which they now pay to the creditors of the State. That the 40 million of taxes being taken off, all productions would be cheaper, and the consumption would considerably increase; that it would give work to the laborer, in place of sabre cuts, which are now dealt out to them; and I confess that these consequences do not appear to me of a nature to terrify the friends of public welfare.

33. Page 498.

34. The manufactured labors which a new state can perform to the greatest .advantage, are in general those of preparing matter from its rough state, or inexpensive commerce. It is not probable that the United States will ever furnish Europe with cloth, but they will perhaps furnish it with manufactured tobacco, and refined sugar: and who knows

that they will not succeed in establishing cotton manufactories at a cheaper rate than England?

35. Considerations on the Policy of Entails, page 14.

36. "When a machine is invented, which by saving manual labor brings the commodities to a lower price the ordinary effect is an increase in the demand, so that the total value of the quantity of commodities thus made far exceeds the total former value of the same commodities; whereby the number of workmen employed in the manufacture is increased rather than diminished." Malthus's *Principles of Political Economy*, page 402.

"But we must admit that the principal advantage arising from the substitution of machines for manual labor. depends upon the extent of the sale. and the encouragement which results from it for consumption, and that without this the advantage of this substitution is all but lost." Page 412.

37. New Principles of Political Economy, vol. 2, page 317.

38. Book 1. Chap. 4.

39. "It is therefore evident that the value of commodities, that is, the sacrifice in labor or in any other article which persons consent to make to obtain them in exchange," etc. Malthus' *Principles of Political Economy*. page 341. English Edition.

40. See the Notes added by me to the French Translation by M. Constance, of Mr. Ricardo's *Principles of Political Economy*.

41. Mr. Ricardo's *Principles of Political Economy*, 2d. English Edition. chap.20.

www.ingramcontent.com/pod-product-compliance
Lightning Source LLC
Chambersburg PA
CBHW022115170526
45157CB00004B/1651